101 THINGS® TO DO WITH A
SMOKER

101 THINGS® TO DO WITH A
SMOKER

ELIZA CROSS

Gibbs Smith

First Edition
27 26 25 24 23   5 4 3 2 1

101 Things is a registered trademark of Gibbs Smith and Stephanie Ashcraft.

Published by
Gibbs Smith
P.O. Box 667
Layton, Utah 84041

1.800.835.4993 orders
www.gibbs-smith.com

Designed by Ryan Thomann and Renee Bond
Printed and bound in China
Gibbs Smith books are printed on either recycled, 100% post-consumer
waste, FSC-certified papers or on paper produced from sustainable PEFC-
certified forest/controlled wood source. Learn more at www.pefc.org.

Library of Congress Cataloging-in-Publication Data has been applied for.
ISBN: 978-1-4236-6245-7

For my great Glencoe friends, the "Flamily"

CONTENTS

Helpful Hints » 8

#1–14 Rubs, Brines & Sauces

All-Around Rub » 12

Rib Rub » 13

Ancho Chili Garlic Rub » 14

Jerk Seasoning » 15

Smoked Salt » 16

Basic Brine » 17

Poultry Brine » 18

Pork Brine » 19

S.P.O.G. Seasoning » 19

Smokin' Good BBQ Sauce » 20

Sticky Peach Barbecue Sauce » 21

Bourbon–Brown Sugar Barbecue Sauce » 22

Smoky Cola Barbecue Sauce » 23

Horseradish Cream » 24

#15–24 Breakfasts

Blueberry Buttermilk Coffee Cake » 26

Bourbon–Brown Sugar Sweet Rolls » 27

Apple-Cinnamon French Toast Bake » 28

Bacon and Hash Brown Breakfast Casserole » 29

Smoked Potato, Pepper, and Sausage Hash » 30

Sausage and Sun-Dried Tomato Mini Frittatas » 31

Smoky Ham and Cheddar Quiche » 32

Smoked Ham and Cheese Breakfast Sliders » 33

Bacon Breakfast Torpedo » 34

Smoked Bacon Candy » 35

#25–35 Sandwiches

Smoked Bratwurst with Ballpark Onions » 38

Smoky Chili Cheese Dogs » 39

Spicy Jerk Chicken Sandwiches » 40

Pulled Pork Sandwiches with Granny's Slaw » 41

Smoked Egg Salad Sandwiches » 42

Smoked Hot Browns » 43

Smoked Ham, Brie, and Cranberry Sliders » 44

Smoky Joes » 45

Bacon-Cheddar Smokehouse Burgers » 46

Smoked Cheesesteak Sandwiches » 47

Smoked Meatball Subs » 48

#36–55 Appetizers & Snacks

Smoked Salsa Queso and Chips » 50

Hot Bacon Dip » 51

Smoky Artichoke Dip » 52

Smoked Hummus » 53

Smoked Hot Wings » 54

Sticky Peach Wings » 55

Smoked Bacon and Sausage Bites » 56

Tex-Mex Smoked Cream Cheese » 57

Smoky Steak Bites » 58

Smoked Bacon-Stuffed Mushrooms » 59

Pulled Pork BBQ Nachos » 60

Burnt End–Style Franks » 61

Roasted Garlic Parmesan Bread » 62

Smoked Bacon and Cheese Potato Skins » 63

Bacon-Jalapeño Poppers » 64

Sweet and Spicy Bacon-
   Wrapped Meatballs » 65

Sticky-Sweet Pork Belly Burnt Ends » 66

Smoked Almonds » 67

Smoky Snack Mix » 68

Smoked Olives » 69

#56–70 Sides & Salads

Smoked Mashed Potatoes » 72

Smoked Corn on the Cob with
   Garlic Chive Butter » 73

Buttery Parmesan Cauliflower » 74

Glazed Smoky Yams » 75

Smoked Green Beans with
   Parmesan Cheese » 76

Smokehouse Brussels Sprouts » 77

Toasty Marshmallow Sweet
   Potatoes » 78

Smoked Twice-Baked Potatoes » 79

Maple-Pecan Butternut Squash » 80

Smoked Bacon Deviled Eggs » 81

Smoky Baked Beans with Bacon » 82

Smoked Turkey Salad » 83

Smoked Italian Pasta Salad » 84

14K Bacon-Wrapped Carrots » 85

Roasted Red Potato Salad
   with Bacon » 86

#71–90 Main Courses

Smoked Prime Rib with
   Horseradish Cream » 88

Easy Homemade Pastrami » 89

Smoky Cheddar Meatloaf » 90

Smoked Beef Short Ribs » 91

Cowpoke Beef Stew » 92

Simple Pulled Pork » 93

Smoked Pork Tenderloin
   Wrapped in Bacon » 94

Smoked Cola-Marinated Pork » 95

Easy Baby Back Ribs » 96

Twice-Smoked Maple-
   Bourbon Ham » 97

Potato, Ham, and Cheese
   Casserole » 98

Smoked Apple Cider Turkey » 99

Easy Smoked Turkey Breast » 100

Smoked Bacon-Wrapped Chicken » 101

Beer Can Butter Chicken » 102

Smoked Trout » 103

Bacon and Green Chile Mac
   and Cheese » 104

Smoked Brown Sugar Salmon » 105

Lemon-Garlic Shrimp » 106

Butter-Basted King Crab Legs » 107

#91–101 Desserts & Sweets

Caramel-Walnut Cheesecake » 110

Smoked Pumpkin Pie » 111

Chocolate-Bourbon Pecan Pie » 112

Apple Pecan Cake » 113

Peach-Bourbon Skillet Upside-
   Down Cake » 114

Smoky Chocolate Ganache Sauce » 115

Smoky Peanut Butter Cup S'mores » 116

Brown Sugar Pineapple » 117

Smoked Cherry Crisp » 118

The Most Appealing Banana
   Dessert » 119

Brown Butter Chocolate
   Chip Cookies » 120

Notes » 122

About the Author » 128

Helpful Hints

- When choosing wood for your smoker, consider how much smoke flavor you want in the finished dish.
  - Milder woods that are commonly available include maple, apple, cherry, peach, and pecan.
  - Moderately flavored woods include walnut and alder.
  - More strongly flavored woods include hickory, mesquite, and oak.
- Whether you're smoking with pellets, disks, chips, or chunks, be sure your wood is dry for the best smoke and temperature control.
- Some foods absorb smoke more easily than others. Chicken, other poultry, and fattier fish tend to absorb smoke, so you may wish to use milder woods when smoking them.
- In general, smoking at a lower temperature will add a more pronounced smoke flavor, while cooking at a higher temperature will add subtle smokiness.
- The recipes in this book use the hot-smoking method. About 30 to 45 minutes before smoking, light or preheat the smoker to the desired temperature according to the manufacturer's instructions. Allow plenty of time for smoking since temperatures can vary throughout the process. For slow-cooked foods with longer cooking times, check the fuel every hour or so and refuel as needed.
- An instant-read food thermometer is a must for smoking meats, poultry, and fish to perfection. For larger cuts of

meat and longer cooking times, use a heat-safe probe thermometer. Always cook foods to the proper internal temperature when specified in the recipe, as cooking times may vary.

- Brining meat or poultry before smoking can help keep it moist and add additional flavor. This cookbook includes several basic brines that are easy to use.

- Spice mixes and rubs add additional flavor. If you prefer to salt the ingredients to your own preference prior to smoking, you can omit the salt from the spice blend and rub recipes.

- Some meats can dry out with long, slow heat exposure. A water pan in the smoker can help maintain humidity. If your smoker doesn't have a built-in water pan, you can simply fill a pan with water and place it in the smoker during cooking. This will also help stabilize the temperature for more even cooking.

- The vents in your smoker can be used to control the cooking temperature. Opening the vents to introduce more air into the smoker will raise the heat and temperature. Adjusting the vents to reduce airflow will lower the heat and temperature.

- A little smoke goes a long way. Cooking with moderate smoke levels will ensure that the flavor is pleasing and not overpowering.

RESOURCES

For detailed information and complete smoking techniques, I recommend these books:

Project Smoke, Steven Raichlen, Workman Publishing Company, 2016.

Smoking Meat 101: The Ultimate Beginner's Guide, Bill West, Rockridge Press, 2019.

Meathead: The Science of Great Barbecue and Grilling, Meathead Goldwyn, Harvest, 2016.

RECIPE NOTES

- Exact cooking times can be affected by many factors, including how hot your smoker heats, the size and thickness of ingredients, fuel used, humidity, how often the smoker is opened, etc. Check foods on the early side of the cooking range and adjust accordingly.

- Using an instant-read thermometer is the best way to ensure the meat is done. When a time range is included, check frequently and adjust accordingly.

- The recipes in this book were tested with large eggs and all-purpose flour. Salt in a recipe refers to table salt unless a recipe specifically calls for kosher salt. (To substitute, 1 tablespoon kosher salt equals approximately 2 teaspoons table salt.) If a specific ingredient is not specified, such as salted or unsalted butter, you can use whichever you like and adjust the seasonings accordingly.

RUBS, BRINES & SAUCES

All-Around Rub

MAKES ABOUT ½ CUP

2 tablespoons	**smoked paprika**
2 tablespoons	**garlic powder**
2 tablespoons	**onion powder**
2 tablespoons	**freshly ground black pepper**
	kosher salt for sprinkling*

In a small bowl, whisk together paprika, garlic powder, onion powder, and pepper. Use as a seasoning rub for poultry, beef, pork, and game. Store in a glass jar in a cool place.

*About 1 hour before the meat goes into the smoker, sprinkle with kosher salt as needed for the size and type of meat. If you prefer a rub that includes salt, add 2 tablespoons kosher salt to the mix.

Rib Rub

MAKES ABOUT 1 CUP

$^2/_3$ cup	packed brown sugar
4 tablespoons	kosher salt
2 tablespoons	chili powder
2 tablespoons	smoked paprika
1 tablespoon	ground cumin
2 teaspoons	freshly ground black pepper
2 teaspoons	garlic powder
2 teaspoons	onion powder
1 teaspoon	dry mustard
$^1/_2$ teaspoon	cayenne pepper

In a medium bowl, whisk together the brown sugar, salt, chili powder, paprika, cumin, pepper, garlic powder, onion powder, mustard, and cayenne.

Use as a dry rub for pork or beef ribs about 1 hour before the meat goes into the smoker. Store in a glass jar in a cool place.

Ancho Chili Garlic Rub

MAKES ABOUT 1 1/2 CUPS

1 cup	**packed dark brown sugar**
1/4 cup	**kosher salt**
2 tablespoons	**coarsely ground black pepper**
2 tablespoons	**regular or smoked paprika**
2 tablespoons	**ancho chili powder**
2 tablespoons	**dry mustard**
1/2 tablespoon	**granulated garlic or garlic powder**
1 teaspoon	**onion powder**

In a medium bowl, whisk together brown sugar, salt, pepper, paprika, chili powder, mustard, garlic, and onion powder. Use as a dry rub for cuts of pork such as shoulder roast, ribs, and tenderloin. Store in a glass jar in a cool place.

Jerk Seasoning

MAKES ABOUT 1/2 CUP

1 tablespoon	onion powder
1 tablespoon	garlic powder
1 tablespoon	ground ginger
1 tablespoon	Scotch bonnet pepper powder or habanero powder
1 tablespoon	packed brown sugar
1 tablespoon	kosher salt
2 teaspoons	dried thyme
1 teaspoon	ground allspice
1/2 teaspoon	ground cumin
1/2 teaspoon	ground cinnamon
1/2 teaspoon	ground nutmeg

In a medium bowl, whisk together onion powder, garlic powder, ginger, Scotch bonnet pepper powder, brown sugar, salt, thyme, allspice, cumin, cinnamon, and nutmeg. Use as a dry rub for chicken, pork, and seafood. Store in a glass jar in a cool place.

Smoked Salt

MAKES 2 CUPS

2 cups   coarse sea salt

Preheat smoker and add wood following the manufacturer's instructions. Heat to 175 degrees F and high smoke setting.

Spread the salt on a rimmed baking pan. Place the pan in the smoker and close the lid. Cook for 3 hours, stirring salt every 30 minutes.

Remove pan from smoker and cool to room temperature. Use salt as a seasoning for beef, poultry, pork, seafood, popcorn, baked potatoes, scrambled eggs, etc. Store in a glass jar in a cool place.

Basic Brine

FINISHED QUANTITY VARIES

For each pound of meat, poultry, or fish:

1	**quart water**
$\frac{1}{2}$ cup	**kosher salt (or $\frac{1}{4}$ cup table salt)**
$\frac{1}{2}$ cup	**sugar**

Optional additions, to taste:

crushed garlic cloves
lemon slices
bay leaves
fresh herb sprigs such as
    tarragon, rosemary, or oregano

Combine the water, salt, and sugar in a container large enough to hold the meat, poultry, or fish completely submerged. Whisk thoroughly until sugar and salt are dissolved. Add any optional ingredients, then add the meat. Cover and refrigerate for about 1 hour per pound of meat. Remove the meat from the brine and rinse with cool water; pat dry with paper towels. Proceed with cooking.

Poultry Brine

MAKES ABOUT 8 3/4 CUPS

8 cups	**water**
1/2 cup	**kosher salt**
1/4 cup	**honey**
3	**dried bay leaves**
3	**garlic cloves, peeled and crushed**
1 tablespoon	**whole black peppercorns**
3	**sprigs fresh thyme**
2	**lemons, sliced**

Place the water, salt, honey, bay leaves, garlic, peppercorns, thyme, and lemons in a large pot. Bring to a simmer over medium heat. Cook, stirring, until salt has dissolved, about 3 to 4 minutes. Remove from heat and cool to room temperature.

Add the poultry to the cooled brine, making sure it is completely submerged. Cover the pot and refrigerate for 8 to 24 hours. Remove poultry from the brine and rinse with cool water; pat dry with paper towels. Proceed with cooking.

Pork Brine

MAKES ABOUT 5 CUPS

4 cups	**water**
1 cup	**packed brown sugar**
$1/4$ cup	**kosher salt**
4	**garlic cloves, peeled and crushed**
$1/2$	**onion, sliced**

Mix water, brown sugar, salt, garlic, and onion in a large bowl until sugar is dissolved. Add pork chops, loin, shoulder, etc. (Double or triple the recipe if needed so that brine completely covers pork.) Cover and refrigerate for at least 2 hours and up to 8 hours. Drain meat, pat dry and proceed with recipe.

S.P.O.G. Seasoning

MAKES ABOUT $1/2$ CUP

$1/4$ cup	**kosher salt**
2 tablespoons	**freshly ground black pepper**
1 tablespoon	**onion powder**
1 tablespoon	**garlic powder**

In a small bowl, whisk together salt, pepper, onion powder, and garlic powder. Use as a general seasoning for all meats and as a dry rub for brisket and steaks. Store in a glass jar in a cool place.

Smokin' Good BBQ Sauce

MAKES ABOUT 4 CUPS

1¹/₂ cups	**packed dark brown sugar**
1¹/₂ cups	**ketchup**
¹/₂ cup	**water**
¹/₃ cup	**red wine vinegar**
1 tablespoon	**Worcestershire sauce**
¹/₂ teaspoon	**liquid smoke flavoring**
¹/₄ teaspoon	**hot pepper sauce**
2 tablespoons	**dry mustard**
2 teaspoons	**smoked paprika**
2 teaspoons	**salt**
1¹/₂ teaspoons	**freshly ground black pepper**

In a medium saucepan, whisk together the brown sugar, ketchup, water, vinegar, Worcestershire sauce, liquid smoke, and hot pepper sauce.

In a small bowl, whisk together the mustard, paprika, salt, and pepper. Add this mixture to the ketchup mixture and whisk until blended. Cook over medium heat, stirring occasionally, just until the mixture bubbles. Remove from heat, cool to room temperature, and use as an accompaniment for all kinds of smoked meats and poultry. Store in a tightly sealed glass container in the refrigerator for up to 1 month.

Sticky Peach Barbecue Sauce
MAKES ABOUT 3 3/4 CUPS

1 cup	1/2-inch chunks peeled ripe peaches
3/4 cup	apple cider vinegar
3/4 cup	maple syrup
1/2 cup	tomato paste
1/2 cup	regular molasses
1/3 cup	water
2 tablespoons	packed brown sugar
1 tablespoon	onion powder
1 teaspoon	garlic powder
2 teaspoons	lemon juice
1/2 teaspoon	salt
1/2 teaspoon	freshly ground black pepper
1/2 teaspoon	ground mustard
1/2 teaspoon	paprika

Combine peaches, vinegar, syrup, tomato paste, molasses, water, brown sugar, onion powder, garlic powder, lemon juice, salt, pepper, mustard, and paprika in a medium saucepan and stir well. Cook over medium heat, stirring frequently, until mixture starts to bubble. Reduce heat to medium-low and cook, stirring often, until sauce thickens and peaches begin to break down (20 to 25 minutes). Remove from heat and cool. Use as a condiment and as a basting sauce for smoking meats and poultry. Store in a tightly sealed glass jar in the refrigerator for up to 2 weeks.

Bourbon–Brown Sugar Barbecue Sauce

MAKES ABOUT 4 CUPS

1 cup	ketchup
1 cup	apple cider vinegar
3/4 cup	regular (not blackstrap) molasses
3/4 cup	packed brown sugar
1/2 cup	honey
1 teaspoon	liquid smoke flavoring
1/2 teaspoon	salt
1/4 teaspoon	freshly ground black pepper
1/4 teaspoon	garlic powder
1/4 teaspoon	onion powder
1/4 teaspoon	hot pepper sauce
1 1/2 tablespoons	bourbon

Combine ketchup, vinegar, molasses, brown sugar, honey, liquid smoke, salt, pepper, garlic powder, onion powder, and hot pepper sauce in a medium saucepan and whisk until well blended. Cook over medium heat until mixture begins to bubble. Reduce heat to low and simmer uncovered, stirring frequently until sauce thickens and coats the back of a spoon, about 1 hour.

Add bourbon, stir to combine, and continue cooking for 5 minutes. Remove from heat and cool to room temperature. Use as a condiment and basting sauce for smoking meats and poultry. Store in a tightly sealed glass jar in the refrigerator for up to 4 weeks.

Smoky Cola Barbecue Sauce
MAKES ABOUT 4 CUPS

1¹⁄₂ cups	packed brown sugar
1¹⁄₂ cups	ketchup
³⁄₄ cup	cola
¹⁄₃ cup	balsamic vinegar
1 tablespoon	Worcestershire sauce
1 teaspoon	liquid smoke flavoring
¹⁄₄ teaspoon	hot pepper sauce
2 tablespoons	dry mustard
2 teaspoons	smoked paprika
2 teaspoons	salt
1¹⁄₂ teaspoons	freshly ground black pepper

Combine brown sugar, ketchup, cola, vinegar, Worcestershire sauce, liquid smoke, and hot pepper sauce in a blender or food processor.

In a small bowl, whisk together the mustard, paprika, salt, and pepper until well combined. Add to the ketchup mixture in the blender and blend on high speed for about 1 minute or until smooth.

Transfer to a saucepan and cook over medium heat, stirring occasionally, until the sauce starts to simmer. Cook for 5 more minutes, stirring frequently. Remove from heat, cool to room temperature, and serve. May be used as a condiment and a basting sauce for smoking and grilling meats and poultry. Store in a tightly sealed glass jar in the refrigerator for up to 6 weeks.

Horseradish Cream

MAKES ABOUT 1 1/2 CUPS

1/2 cup	heavy whipping cream, chilled
1/4 cup	prepared horseradish
2 tablespoons	mayonnaise
2 teaspoons	Dijon mustard
1/4 teaspoon	salt
1/4 teaspoon	freshly ground black pepper
1/8 teaspoon	sugar

In the bowl of a stand mixer or in a mixing bowl with an electric mixer, beat the whipping cream on medium-high speed until soft peaks form; set aside.

In a medium bowl, stir together the horseradish, mayonnaise, mustard, salt, pepper, and sugar until well combined. Gently fold the horseradish mixture into the whipped cream until combined. Serve as an accompaniment to smoked and grilled meats, or as a dipping sauce or general condiment. Store in the refrigerator and use within 2 days (whisk to recombine before serving if needed).

BREAKFASTS

Blueberry Buttermilk Coffee Cake

MAKES 6 SERVINGS

For the streusel topping:

1/4 cup	flour
1/4 cup	packed brown sugar
2 tablespoons	butter, softened
1/2 teaspoon	cinnamon
1/4 cup	chopped pecans

For the coffee cake:

2 cups	flour
1 tablespoon	baking powder
3/4 teaspoon	baking soda
1/4 teaspoon	salt
1/2 cup	sugar
2	eggs
1 cup	buttermilk
1/4 cup	butter, melted
1/2 cup	fresh or frozen blueberries

Preheat smoker and add wood following the manufacturer's instructions. Heat to 350 degrees F. Grease an 8-inch square metal baking pan.

For the streusel topping, combine the flour, brown sugar, butter, cinnamon, and pecans in a small bowl and stir with a fork until crumbly; set aside.

For the coffee cake, whisk together the flour, baking powder, baking soda, and salt in a large bowl. In a separate bowl, whisk together the sugar, eggs, buttermilk, and melted butter until smooth. Pour the egg mixture into the flour mixture and stir just until combined (do not overmix). Spread the batter in the prepared baking pan and sprinkle with blueberries. Sprinkle with streusel topping. Place the baking pan in the center of the smoker, close the lid, and cook until the top is golden brown and a toothpick inserted comes out clean, 40 to 50 minutes. Cool, cut into squares, and serve.

#16

Bourbon–Brown Sugar Sweet Rolls

MAKES 12 SERVINGS

³/₄ **cup**	**butter, melted**
1 cup	**packed dark brown sugar**
¹/₄ **cup**	**bourbon**
2 cans (17.5 ounces)	**jumbo refrigerated cinnamon rolls**

Preheat smoker and add wood following the manufacturer's instructions. Heat to 350 degrees F.

Pour melted butter into a 12-inch cast iron skillet. Sprinkle with the brown sugar, add the bourbon, and whisk until smooth. Arrange the cinnamon rolls in the skillet, reserving the icing. Place in the middle rack of the smoker over indirect heat, close the lid, and cook until rolls are cooked through and lightly browned, 30 to 45 minutes.

Remove skillet from smoker and cool for 5 minutes. Cover skillet with a serving plate and flip over to remove rolls. Drizzle with reserved icing.

Apple-Cinnamon French Toast Bake

MAKES 6 SERVINGS

1 pound	day-old challah or French bread, cut into 1-inch cubes
2	large Granny Smith apples, peeled and chopped
1 cup	packed brown sugar
2 teaspoons	cornstarch
6	eggs
1 cup	half-and-half
1 cup	milk
1 teaspoon	vanilla
1 teaspoon	cinnamon
1/4 teaspoon	nutmeg
1/4 cup	maple syrup
	powdered sugar for sprinkling

Preheat smoker and add wood following the manufacturer's instructions. Heat to 350 degrees F. Grease a 9 x 13-inch metal baking pan.

In a medium bowl, combine the bread cubes, apples, brown sugar, and cornstarch. In a separate medium bowl, whisk together the eggs, half-and-half, milk, vanilla, cinnamon, and nutmeg. Pour the egg mixture into the bread bowl and stir well until all the mixture is absorbed by the bread.

Spread into the prepared baking pan. Drizzle the top evenly with maple syrup. Place in the middle rack of the smoker, put the lid down, and cook until filling is set and top is golden brown, 45 to 60 minutes. Sprinkle with powdered sugar and serve warm.

Bacon and Hash Brown Breakfast Casserole

MAKES 6 SERVINGS

30 ounces	frozen hash browns, thawed
1 pound	smoked bacon, cooked, drained, and crumbled
1	small sweet onion such as Vidalia, chopped
12	large eggs
1 teaspoon	salt
1/2 teaspoon	freshly ground black pepper
1 cup	whole milk
3/4 cup	shredded sharp cheddar cheese
3/4 cup	shredded Monterey Jack cheese chopped flat-leaf parsley for garnish

Preheat smoker and add wood following the manufacturer's instructions. Heat to 350 degrees F. Grease a 9 x 13-inch metal baking pan.

Spread the hash browns evenly in bottom of pan. Sprinkle with the crumbled bacon and onion.

In a large bowl, whisk together the eggs, salt, pepper, and milk. Pour over the hash brown mixture and sprinkle with the cheeses. Place in the middle rack of the smoker over indirect heat, close the lid, and cook until the eggs are set, 45 to 60 minutes. Garnish with chopped parsley and cut into squares.

Smoked Potato, Pepper, and Sausage Hash

MAKES 6 SERVINGS

12 ounces	**bulk breakfast sausage**
1¹/₂ tablespoons	**extra virgin olive oil**
3	**large Yukon Gold potatoes, peeled and cubed**
¹/₂ teaspoon	**salt**
¹/₄ teaspoon	**freshly ground black pepper**
1	**small sweet onion, chopped**
¹/₂	**large red bell pepper, seeded and chopped**
1	**large Anaheim chile, seeded and chopped**
2	**garlic cloves, peeled and minced**

Preheat smoker and add wood following the manufacturer's instructions. Heat to 350 degrees F.

In a large cast iron skillet, cook the breakfast sausage on the stovetop over medium heat, breaking up with a spatula, until browned. Use a slotted spoon to transfer sausage to paper towels to drain. Pour out all but 1 tablespoon drippings. Add the olive oil and swirl to blend. Add the cubed potatoes, stir to coat with the oil, and sprinkle with salt and pepper.

Place the skillet on the smoker grill grates, close the lid, and cook until potatoes are just starting to brown on the bottom, 7 to 14 minutes. Stir, add the onion, and cook for another 5 minutes. Add the bell pepper, chile, garlic, and reserved sausage to the skillet and stir.

Return to the smoker and cook until the potatoes are browned and peppers are tender, stirring occasionally, 20 to 30 more minutes. Remove from smoker, cool for 5 minutes, and serve.

Sausage and Sun-Dried Tomato Mini Frittatas

MAKES 12 SERVINGS

¹/₂ pound	**ground pork sausage**
1	**small onion, chopped**
12	**eggs, beaten**
¹/₃ cup	**milk**
¹/₃ cup	**sun-dried tomatoes in oil, drained and finely chopped**
1 teaspoon	**garlic powder**
¹/₄ teaspoon	**salt**
¹/₈ teaspoon	**pepper**
1 cup	**shredded cheddar cheese, divided fresh basil leaves for garnish**

Preheat smoker and add wood following the manufacturer's instructions. Heat to 350 degrees F.

Grease a metal 12-cup muffin pan.

In a large skillet, cook sausage on the stovetop over medium-high heat until browned. Transfer with a slotted spoon to paper towels to drain. Pour out all but 2 teaspoons drippings, add the onion and cook over medium heat until translucent, about 5 minutes; set aside.

In a large bowl, combine eggs, milk, sun-dried tomatoes, garlic powder, salt, pepper, sausage, onion, and ¹/₂ cup cheese and mix well. Spoon about ¹/₄ cup of sausage mixture into each prepared muffin cup and sprinkle with remaining ¹/₂ cup cheese. Place in the middle rack of the smoker and close the lid. Cook until the egg has set in the middle of the frittatas, 20 to 30 minutes. Cool for 5 minutes, loosen edges with a sharp knife, and garnish with fresh basil.

Smoky Ham and Cheddar Quiche

MAKES 6 SERVINGS

1 (9-inch)	uncooked pie crust
6	eggs, beaten
1 cup	half-and-half
1/4 teaspoon	salt
1/4 teaspoon	freshly ground black pepper
1 cup	shredded extra sharp cheddar cheese
1/2 cup	diced smoked Black Forest ham
2 tablespoons	finely chopped pimientos, drained
1 tablespoon	finely chopped fresh chives or green onion

Preheat smoker and add wood following the manufacturer's instructions. Heat to 350 degrees F. Place the pie crust in the smoker, put the lid down, and smoke for 10 minutes. Meanwhile, combine the eggs, half-and-half, salt, and pepper in a medium bowl and whisk to combine. Stir in the cheese, ham, and pimientos.

Remove the pie crust from the smoker, pour in the egg mixture, and return it to the smoker. Close the lid and cook until the filling is set, 45 to 60 minutes. Cool for 5 minutes. Garnish with chives or green onions, cut into wedges, and serve.

Smoked Ham and Cheese Breakfast Sliders

MAKE 12 SERVINGS

24	Hawaiian rolls (about 1 1/2 packages)
12	eggs, beaten
1 pound	thinly sliced smoked ham
12 slices	American cheese
1/4 cup	butter, melted
1/4 cup	maple syrup

Preheat smoker and add wood following the manufacturer's instructions. Heat to 350 degrees F. Grease a 9 x 13-inch metal or disposable aluminum baking pan.

Using a sharp serrated knife, cut Hawaiian rolls in half horizontally without separating the rolls. Arrange the roll bottoms in the prepared baking pan.

In a medium skillet over medium heat, scramble the eggs until cooked but still moist; set aside. Arrange the ham slices evenly over the bottom half of the rolls. Spoon the scrambled eggs over the ham, layer with cheese slices, and top with the upper half of the rolls. Whisk together butter and maple syrup in a small bowl and drizzle the mixture over the rolls. Cover with aluminum foil and place pan on the middle rack of the smoker. Put the lid down and cook for 10 minutes. Remove foil and cook until hot and lightly browned, 10 to 20 more minutes.

Bacon Breakfast Torpedo

MAKES 6 SERVINGS

1¹⁄₂ pounds	regular sliced (not thick cut) bacon
15 ounces (¹⁄₂ bag)	frozen hash browns, thawed
2 teaspoons	All-Around Rub (page 12), divided
1 pound	bulk breakfast sausage
2 cups	shredded sharp cheddar cheese
3	eggs, beaten
¹⁄₃ cup	barbecue sauce

Preheat smoker and add wood following the manufacturer's instructions. Heat to 275 degrees F.

Lay 6 slices of bacon lengthwise and just touching on a square piece of parchment paper. Use 6 more bacon strips to weave over and under the strips, forming a tight square. Chop remaining bacon and fry in a large skillet over medium heat until crisp. Drain on paper towels and pour out all but 1 tablespoon of drippings. Add the hash browns to skillet in an even layer and cook over medium heat, without stirring, until bottom is browned, about 7 minutes. Flip the hash browns and continue cooking until browned; set aside.

Sprinkle bacon weave with 1 teaspoon rub. Spread evenly with sausage, leaving a 1-inch border on the sides. Sprinkle with the cooked bacon. Spread the hash browns on top and sprinkle with cheese. In a medium nonstick skillet, cook the eggs over medium heat, stirring, until softly scrambled. Spoon the eggs on top of the cheese. Roll the torpedo in a cylinder, pinching together the seam and tucking under the ends. Sprinkle with remaining 1 teaspoon rub.

Transfer to a baking sheet and place on the middle rack in the smoker. Close the lid and cook until internal temperature reaches 165 degrees F, about 1$^1/_2$ hours. Brush with the barbecue sauce and cook for 15 more minutes. Cool for 10 minutes, slice, and serve.

#24

Smoked Bacon Candy

MAKES 6 SERVINGS

$^1/_2$ **cup**	**packed dark brown sugar**
$^1/_2$ **cup**	**real maple syrup**
$^1/_4$ **teaspoon**	**freshly ground black pepper**
$^1/_4$ **teaspoon**	**cayenne pepper**
1 pound	**thick-cut bacon**

Preheat smoker and add wood following the manufacturer's instructions. Heat to 275 degrees F. Line a baking sheet with aluminum foil. Spray with nonstick cooking spray.

Combine the brown sugar, maple syrup, black pepper, and cayenne in a shallow bowl. Whisk together until combined. Dip each piece of bacon in the glaze and arrange the strips on the prepared baking sheet.

Put the baking sheet in the smoker, close lid, and cook for 20 minutes. Turn the bacon strips over, blot excess grease from the pan with paper towels, and continue cooking until bacon is glazed and browned, 20 to 40 minutes. Cool bacon in pan for 10 minutes, blot excess grease with paper towels and serve.

SANDWICHES

Smoked Bratwurst with Ballpark Onions

MAKES 6 SERVINGS

6	bratwurst sausages
1 tablespoon	vegetable oil
1 tablespoon	butter
1	large yellow onion, quartered and cut into $1/4$-inch slices
$1/2$ cup	chicken stock or broth
2 tablespoons	tomato paste
1 teaspoon	yellow mustard
1 teaspoon	hot pepper sauce
1 teaspoon	sugar
1 teaspoon	salt
$1/4$ teaspoon	freshly ground black pepper
6	hot dog buns, lightly toasted

Preheat smoker and add wood following the manufacturer's instructions. Heat to 275 degrees F. Lightly brush the brats with the oil to prevent sticking. Arrange on the smoking rack, close the lid, and smoke until the sausages are bubbling and cooked through and an instant-read thermometer reads 155 degrees F, 45 to 55 minutes, turning several times during smoking.

While brats are cooking, melt the butter in a large skillet over medium heat and add the sliced onion. Cook, stirring occasionally, until onion is tender and translucent, about 6 minutes. Add the chicken stock, tomato paste, mustard, hot sauce, sugar, salt, and pepper, and stir until combined. Continue cooking until mixture thickens, 20 to 25 minutes. Remove from heat and set aside.

When brats are done, remove from smoker and serve in toasted buns with some of the onions spooned on top.

Smoky Chili Cheese Dogs

MAKES 8 SERVINGS

1 pound	lean ground beef
1	large yellow onion diced, divided
2	garlic cloves, minced
1 can (28 ounces)	tomato sauce
1$^1/_2$ tablespoons	chili powder
2 teaspoons	ground cumin
1 teaspoon	salt
8	bun length all-beef hot dogs
8 slices	American cheese, cut in half
8	hot dog buns, toasted

Preheat smoker and add wood following the manufacturer's instructions. Heat to 225 degrees F.

In a large cast iron skillet, cook the ground beef on the stovetop over medium heat until browned. Drain excess grease and add $^3/_4$ of the onion to the skillet, reserving the rest for garnish. Cook until onion is tender, about 5 minutes. Add garlic and cook, stirring constantly, for 1 minute. Add tomato sauce, chili powder, cumin, and salt and cook for 5 minutes, stirring occasionally.

Place the skillet in the lower rack of the smoker. Arrange the hot dogs in a metal baking pan and place in the middle rack of the smoker. Close the lid and smoke for 1 hour.

Lay 2 half-slices of cheese on each dog lengthwise and continue cooking until melted, about 5 minutes. To assemble, place toasted buns on plates, top each with a cheese-covered hot dog, and spoon some of the chili over the top. Sprinkle with reserved chopped onions.

Spicy Jerk Chicken Sandwiches

MAKES 6 SERVINGS

1/4 cup	orange juice
1/4 cup	apple cider vinegar
2 tablespoons	soy sauce
2 tablespoons	olive oil
2 tablespoons	lime juice
1/2 cup	Jerk Seasoning (page 15), divided
2 pounds	boneless chicken breasts
6	onion buns, split and toasted
2 tablespoons	mayonnaise
	lettuce leaves
	dill pickle slices

In a medium bowl, whisk together the orange juice, vinegar, soy sauce, olive oil, lime juice, and 1/3 cup Jerk Seasoning. Pour the mixture into a large resealable bag, add the chicken, seal, and refrigerate for 4 hours, turning occasionally.

Preheat smoker and add wood following the manufacturer's instructions. Heat to 225 degrees F.

Remove chicken from marinade, shaking off excess, and discard marinade. Sprinkle the chicken with the remaining Jerk Seasoning and arrange pieces directly on grill grates. Close the lid and smoke until the internal temperature at the thickest part of the chicken reaches 165 degrees F, 1 1/2 to 2 hours. Cool for 5 minutes and cut into 1-inch strips.

Spread the bottom buns with mayonnaise and top with lettuce. Divide the chicken among the sandwiches and top with pickle slices. Top with upper buns and serve.

Pulled Pork Sandwiches with Granny's Slaw

MAKES 6 SERVINGS

¹/₃ cup	mayonnaise
2 tablespoons	dill pickle juice from pickle jar
1¹/₂ teaspoons	balsamic vinegar
1 teaspoon	sugar
¹/₈ teaspoon	salt
¹/₄ teaspoon	freshly ground black pepper
¹/₄ teaspoon	dry mustard
1	medium dill pickle, finely chopped (about 2 tablespoons)
2 cups	bagged coleslaw mix
3 cups	Simple Pulled Pork (page 93)
³/₄ cup	Smokin' Good BBQ Sauce (page 20) or your favorite sauce
6	large sesame buns, split and toasted

In a medium bowl, whisk together the mayonnaise, pickle juice, vinegar, sugar, salt, pepper, and mustard until smooth. Add the dill pickle and coleslaw mix, and toss to coat. (Slaw may be prepared in advance. Cover and refrigerate for up to 2 days.)

In a large skillet, heat the pulled pork until warm. Drizzle with the barbecue sauce and stir until heated through. Divide the pulled pork between the 6 bottom buns and top with a generous spoonful of the slaw. Top with the upper buns and serve.

Smoked Egg Salad Sandwiches

MAKES 6 SERVINGS

12	hard-boiled eggs, peeled
2/3 cup	mayonnaise
2 teaspoons	yellow mustard
1/2 teaspoon	salt
1/2 teaspoon	freshly ground black pepper
1/2 cup	finely chopped celery
1 tablespoon	dill relish
12 slices	potato bread
6	crisp lettuce leaves

Preheat smoker and add wood following the manufacturer's instructions. Heat to 175 degrees F.

Place the peeled hard-boiled eggs on the grill grates over indirect heat and smoke for 30 minutes. Remove from the smoker and cool in the refrigerator for 15 minutes.

Meanwhile, combine the mayonnaise, mustard, salt, and pepper and whisk until smooth. Add the celery and relish, and mix well. Chop the eggs finely and add to the mayonnaise mixture. Cover and refrigerate for 30 minutes.

To make the sandwiches, divide the egg salad among 6 pieces of bread and spread to the edges. Top with lettuce and remaining bread slices. Cut on the diagonal and serve.

Smoked Hot Browns

MAKES 4 SERVINGS

1 tablespoon	butter
1 tablespoon	flour
1 cup	half-and-half, plus more if needed
1 cup	shredded sharp cheddar cheese
	salt and freshly ground black pepper, to taste
4 slices	Texas toast bread, toasted and buttered
8 slices (¼ inch thick)	smoked turkey breast, room temperature
1	large tomato, thinly sliced
	smoked paprika for sprinkling
¼ cup	shredded Parmesan cheese
6 strips	thick-sliced bacon, cooked, drained, and crumbled

Preheat smoker and add wood following the manufacturer's instructions. Heat to 375 degrees F. Line a baking sheet with aluminum foil and spray with nonstick cooking spray.

Melt butter in a medium saucepan over medium heat. Sprinkle with flour, whisk to combine, and cook for 1 minute. Reduce temperature to medium-low and slowly pour in the half-and-half, whisking constantly until mixture thickens and starts to bubble. Add the cheese and stir until melted, adding additional half-and-half if needed, and seasoning with salt and pepper.

Arrange toast on prepared baking sheet and top with 2 turkey slices each followed by the tomato slices. Ladle the sauce evenly over the 4 sandwiches and sprinkle with smoked paprika and Parmesan cheese. Put the baking sheet in the smoker, close the lid, and smoke until hot and bubbly, 15 to 20 minutes. Sprinkle the bacon over the sandwiches and cook for 5 more minutes.

Smoked Ham, Brie, and Cranberry Sliders

MAKES 6 SERVINGS

1	**(12-pack) Hawaiian rolls**
¹⁄₂ cup	**whole cranberry sauce, room temperature**
¹⁄₂ pound	**sliced smoked ham**
1 wheel (8 ounces)	**Brie cheese, cut in ¹⁄₄-inch slices**
4 tablespoons	**butter, melted**
2 tablespoons	**packed brown sugar**
1 tablespoon	**Dijon mustard**
1 tablespoon	**Worcestershire sauce**
¹⁄₂ teaspoon	**salt**
¹⁄₂ teaspoon	**freshly ground black pepper**

Preheat smoker and add wood following the manufacturer's instructions. Heat to 350 degrees F and grease a 9 x 13-inch metal baking pan.

Slice the pack of Hawaiian rolls horizontally without separating. Place the bottom half of the rolls in the baking pan and spread with the cranberry sauce. Arrange ham slices on top followed by Brie slices. Place the upper half of rolls on top.

In a small bowl, whisk together the butter, brown sugar, mustard, Worcestershire sauce, salt, and pepper until smooth. Drizzle and brush mixture on top of rolls. Place the pan in smoker, close the lid, and cook until cheese is melted, 20 to 25 minutes. Remove pan and cool for 5 minutes. Cut into 12 individual sliders and serve.

Smoky Joes

MAKES 8 SERVINGS

1¹/₂ pounds	lean ground beef
1 tablespoon	All-Around Rub (page 12) or your favorite rub
1 tablespoon	olive oil
1	medium onion, diced
1	red bell pepper, diced
1	garlic clove, minced
2¹/₂ cups	tomato sauce
¹/₃ cup	packed brown sugar
2 tablespoons	tomato paste
1 tablespoon	apple cider vinegar
1 tablespoon	Worcestershire sauce
	salt, to taste
8	sesame hamburger buns, toasted

Preheat smoker and add wood following the manufacturer's instructions. Heat to 200 degrees F and line a rimmed baking sheet with aluminum foil.

Spread the ground beef on the baking sheet and sprinkle with the rub. Put in the smoker, close lid, and smoke for 30 minutes.

Heat the olive oil in a large skillet over medium heat and add the onion, bell pepper, and garlic. Cook, stirring occasionally, until onion and bell pepper are tender, 7 to 8 minutes. Add the smoked ground beef to the skillet and continue cooking, breaking up meat with a spatula, for 10 minutes. Add the tomato sauce, brown sugar, tomato paste, vinegar, Worcestershire sauce, and salt. Bring to a simmer and cook until sauce thickens, about 10 more minutes. Spoon the mixture on the toasted bottom buns, top with upper buns, and serve.

Bacon-Cheddar Smokehouse Burgers

MAKES 6 SERVINGS

2 pounds	**80% lean ground beef chuck**
2 teaspoons	**salt**
2 teaspoons	**freshly ground black pepper**
$1/2$ teaspoon	**onion powder**
$1/2$ teaspoon	**garlic powder**
6 slices	**Colby cheese**
9 strips	**thick-cut bacon, cooked, drained, and cut in half**
6	**hamburger buns, toasted**
2	**large tomatoes, thinly sliced**
1	**large red onion, sliced**
6	**leaves crisp lettuce ketchup, mayonnaise, and mustard, to taste**

Preheat smoker and add wood following the manufacturer's instructions. Heat to 225 degrees F.

In a large bowl, combine the ground beef, salt, pepper, onion powder, and garlic powder. Mix with hands just until combined. Form the mixture in 6 ($1/2$-inch-thick) patties. Place the patties on the grill grates and smoke the burgers until they reach an internal temperature of 150 to 160 degrees F (depending on your desired doneness), 60 to 90 minutes. Top each burger with a cheese slice and 3 half-strips bacon during the last 15 minutes of cooking.

Serve on buns topped with tomatoes, onion, lettuce, ketchup, mayonnaise, and mustard.

Smoked Cheesesteak Sandwiches

MAKES 6 SERVINGS

2 pounds	rib eye steaks
2	medium yellow onions, thinly sliced
2	green bell peppers, thinly sliced
1 tablespoon	olive oil
1 teaspoon	garlic powder
1 teaspoon	salt
1 teaspoon	freshly ground black pepper
9 slices	provolone cheese
6	hoagie rolls, split and toasted
3 cups	beef au jus or broth, heated

Put the steaks in the freezer for 20 minutes. Remove, 1 at a time, and slice very thinly with a sharp knife; set aside.

Preheat smoker and add wood following the manufacturer's instructions. Heat to 275 degrees F.

Spread the sliced beef in half of a 9 x 13-inch metal baking pan. Spread the onions and peppers on the other half. Drizzle with the olive oil, sprinkle with garlic powder, salt, and pepper, and toss to blend with tongs, keeping meat and vegetables separated. Place the pan in smoker, close the lid, and cook until meat is cooked and vegetables are tender, about 1 hour, stirring every 20 minutes during cooking.

Use tongs to combine steak with onions and peppers and spread evenly in pan. Top with cheese slices and return to smoker until cheese is melted, 6 to 10 minutes. Use a spatula to divide the mixture among the rolls and serve with au jus for dipping.

Smoked Meatball Subs

MAKES 6 SERVINGS

1 tablespoon	butter
1/4 cup	finely chopped onion
2	garlic cloves, minced
1/2 pound	bulk Italian sausage
1/2 pound	ground beef chuck
1/3 cup	Italian-seasoned breadcrumbs
1 teaspoon	salt
1/4 teaspoon	freshly ground black pepper
1	egg, lightly beaten
6	sub rolls, split and toasted
1 1/2 cups	marinara sauce, heated
1 cup	shredded mozzarella cheese
1/2 cup	shredded Parmesan cheese

Preheat smoker and add wood following the manufacturer's instructions. Heat to 375 degrees F. Line a baking sheet with aluminum foil and spray with cooking spray.

Heat the butter in a small skillet over medium heat, add the onion and cook until translucent, about 5 minutes. Add the garlic and cook, stirring constantly, for 90 seconds. Remove from heat and cool for 5 minutes.

In a large bowl, mix together the sausage, ground beef, bread-crumbs, salt, and pepper. Add the onion mixture and egg, and stir until well blended. Use a tablespoon to form golf ball-size balls. Arrange on the prepared baking sheet, put in center rack of the smoker, close lid, and smoke until meatballs are cooked and lightly browned, 30 to 40 minutes. Cool for 10 minutes.

To assemble, arrange 3 to 4 meatballs on each roll. Spoon some of the marinara sauce over top and sprinkle with mozzarella and Parmesan cheese.

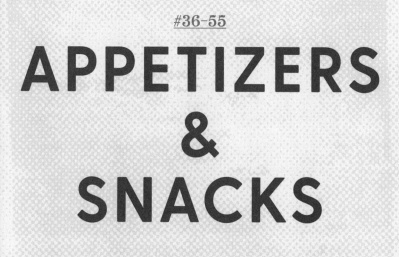

#36–55

APPETIZERS & SNACKS

Smoked Salsa Queso and Chips

MAKES 10 SERVINGS

1/2 pound	bulk chorizo sausage
1/2	large sweet onion such as Vidalia, diced
1	large tomato, cut into 1/4-inch dice
2	jalapeños, seeded and minced
20 ounces	processed American cheese like Velveeta, cut into 1/2-inch cubes
2/3 cup	sour cream
2 tablespoons	chopped cilantro
	yellow and blue tortilla chips

Preheat smoker and add wood following the manufacturer's instructions. Heat to 250 degrees F. Grease an 8 x 8-inch metal or disposable aluminum baking pan. In a large skillet over medium heat, break up the chorizo with a spatula and cook until browned, about 10 minutes. Drain on paper towels and spread in the prepared pan.

Add the chopped onion, tomato, jalapeños, and cheese to pan and stir to mix. Place in the smoker, close the lid, and cook for 1 hour. Remove from heat, stir to incorporate melted cheese, add the sour cream, and stir until creamy and well blended. Return to the smoker and cook until hot, about 20 more minutes. Remove pan from smoker and cool for 5 minutes. Sprinkle with chopped cilantro and serve hot with tortilla chips.

#37
Hot Bacon Dip
MAKES 10 SERVINGS

1 cup	mayonnaise
1 cup	sour cream
8 ounces	cream cheese, softened
1 cup	shredded sharp cheddar cheese
$^1/_3$ cup	grated Parmesan cheese
2	green onions, finely chopped
1 pound	bacon, cooked, drained, and crumbled
1 jar (4 ounces)	diced pimientos, drained assorted crackers or corn chips

Preheat smoker and add wood following the manufacturer's instructions. Heat to 350 degrees F. Grease an 8 x 8-inch metal baking pan.

In medium bowl, combine mayonnaise, sour cream, cheeses, and green onions and stir to combine. Fold in bacon and pimientos and spread into prepared baking pan.

Place on the middle rack of the smoker, close the lid, and smoke until hot and bubbling, 30 to 40 minutes. Remove from smoker, cool for 5 minutes, and serve hot with crackers or corn chips.

Smoky Artichoke Dip

MAKES 12 SERVINGS

2 cans (14 ounces each)	**quartered artichoke hearts, drained and chopped**
1¹/₂ cups	**mayonnaise**
1¹/₂ cups	**shredded Monterey jack cheese**
1¹/₂ cups	**shredded Parmesan cheese**
3	**green onions, finely chopped**
2	**garlic cloves, peeled and minced**
	pita chips for dipping

Preheat smoker and add wood following the manufacturer's instructions. Heat to 350 degrees F. Grease a 9 x 13-inch metal baking pan.

In a large bowl, combine the artichoke hearts, mayonnaise, cheeses, green onions, and garlic. Stir until well blended. Spread into the prepared baking pan.

Place the pan inside the smoker and close the lid. Cook until mixture is hot and bubbling, 30 to 40 minutes. If you wish, you can also smoke the pita chips by spreading them on a baking pan and cooking in the smoker for about 20 minutes. Cool dip for 10 minutes and serve with pita chips for dipping.

Smoked Hummus

MAKES 6 SERVINGS

1 can (15 ounces)	garbanzo beans, drained
4	unpeeled garlic cloves
1¹/₂ tablespoons	fresh lemon juice
2 tablespoons	sesame seeds
1¹/₂ teaspoons	chili powder
1 teaspoon	salt
¹/₄ teaspoon	ground white pepper
¹/₄ cup	extra virgin olive oil, plus extra for drizzling
	assorted sliced raw vegetables

Preheat smoker and add wood following the manufacturer's instructions. Heat to 225 degrees F.

Lightly grease an 8 x 8-inch metal baking pan and add the garbanzo beans, spreading in an even layer. Put 1 garlic clove in each corner of the pan. Place the pan on the smoker grill grates, close the lid, and smoke for 40 minutes. Remove the pan from the smoker and cool for 15 minutes. Peel the garlic and roughly chop.

Add the garbanzo beans, garlic, lemon juice, sesame seeds, chili powder, salt, and white pepper to the bowl of a food processor and pulse until blended. Process and add the oil in a thin stream until mixture is smooth and creamy. Spoon into a serving bowl and drizzle with olive oil. Serve with raw vegetables.

Smoked Hot Wings

MAKES 6 SERVINGS

2 1/2 pounds	chicken wing flats and drumettes
2 tablespoons	All-Around Rub (page 12) or your favorite rub
2/3 cup	hot pepper sauce
1/2 cup	butter
1 1/2 tablespoons	white vinegar
1/2 teaspoon	Worcestershire sauce
1/4 teaspoon	garlic powder
1/4 teaspoon	salt

Pat the wings dry with a paper towel and arrange on a wire baking rack set over a baking sheet. (Drying the wings helps them absorb the smoke.) Refrigerate, uncovered, for 3 hours.

Preheat smoker and add wood following the manufacturer's instructions. Heat to 225 degrees F. Grease a rimmed metal baking sheet.

Sprinkle the chicken wings with the rub and arrange on the prepared baking sheet. Place the baking sheet inside the smoker and close the lid. Smoke the wings for 30 minutes. Turn over and continue cooking for 30 more minutes. Turn over again and increase the heat to 450 degrees F. Continue cooking until an instant-read thermometer inserted near the bone reads 165 degrees F, 15 to 30 more minutes.

Meanwhile, combine hot pepper sauce, butter, vinegar, Worcestershire sauce, garlic powder, and salt in a small saucepan over low heat. Cook, stirring often, until butter is melted and sauce is smooth. Remove from heat.

Remove wings from smoker, transfer to a large bowl, and drizzle with the sauce, stirring to coat.

Sticky Peach Wings

MAKES 8 SERVINGS

3 pounds	chicken wing flats and drumettes
2 tablespoons	All-Around Rub (page 12) or your favorite rub
	vegetable oil, for oiling the rack
1 cup	peach preserves
2 tablespoons	honey
1 tablespoon	balsamic vinegar
1 tablespoon	soy sauce
1	garlic clove, minced
¼ teaspoon	salt
¼ teaspoon	freshly ground black pepper

Put the wings in a large bowl and sprinkle all over with rub, tossing to coat. Cover the bowl and refrigerate for 60 minutes.

Add wood to the smoker following the manufacturer's instructions. Oil the smoker rack and arrange the wings on the cold rack. Heat the smoker to 375 degrees F. After 30 minutes, flip the wings and continue cooking until the internal temperature of the wings is about 175 degrees F, 20 to 35 more minutes. Remove from smoker and cool for 3 minutes.

While wings are cooking, combine the peach preserves, honey, vinegar, soy sauce, garlic, salt, and pepper in a small saucepan and cook over medium heat, stirring, until mixture bubbles and thickens slightly, about 8 minutes. Remove from heat, cover, and set aside until the wings are done.

In a large bowl, toss the hot wings with the peach sauce until coated. Transfer to a serving platter.

Smoked Bacon and Sausage Bites

MAKES 12 SERVINGS

2 links (14 ounces each)	**kielbasa**
1 pound	**regular-sliced bacon**
1/3 cup	**All-Around Rub (page 12) or your favorite rub**
1/2 cup	**packed brown sugar**

Preheat smoker and add wood following the manufacturer's instructions. Heat to 300 degrees F. Line a baking sheet with aluminum foil.

Slice the kielbasa into 1-inch pieces. Wrap each piece with 1/3 slice of bacon and secure with a toothpick. Arrange on the prepared baking sheet and sprinkle with rub. Sprinkle with brown sugar, pressing with fingers to adhere.

Put the baking sheet in the smoker, close the lid, and cook for 20 minutes. Blot bacon grease with paper towels and flip pieces over. Continue cooking until kielbasa is sizzling and bacon is browned, 15 to 25 more minutes. Remove baking sheet, cool for 10 minutes, and serve warm.

Tex-Mex Smoked Cream Cheese

MAKES 6 SERVINGS

1 block (8 ounces)	cream cheese, chilled
1 tablespoon	extra virgin olive oil
1 tablespoon	taco seasoning
1/2 teaspoon	garlic powder
	tortilla chips and salsa for dipping

Preheat smoker and add wood following the manufacturer's instructions. Heat to 200 degrees F.

Place the block of cream cheese on a piece of aluminum foil and freeze for 10 minutes. Remove to a work surface, keeping the cheese on the foil, and brush the top and sides with the olive oil. Sprinkle with taco seasoning and garlic powder, patting mixture gently to adhere to top and sides.

Using a sharp knife, make 1/4-inch-deep cuts 1 inch apart in a diagonal checkerboard pattern on the top of the cheese. Place the cheese on the foil inside an 8 x 8-inch metal baking pan or small disposable aluminum pan. Place in the smoker over indirect heat, close the lid, and smoke for 2 hours. Remove from smoker and serve hot from the pan with tortilla chips and salsa.

Smoky Steak Bites

MAKES 12 SERVINGS

1/3 cup	tamari or low-sodium soy sauce
2 tablespoons	olive oil
1/4 cup	finely chopped onion
4	garlic cloves, minced
2 teaspoons	smoked paprika
1 teaspoon	dried oregano
1 teaspoon	salt
1/2 teaspoon	freshly ground black pepper
3 pounds	beef rib eye, cut into 1 1/4-inch pieces
1/2 cup	butter, melted
	chopped flat-leaf parsley for garnish
	Horseradish Cream (page 24) for dipping

In a large bowl, combine the tamari, olive oil, onion, garlic, paprika, oregano, salt, and pepper, and stir to mix. Add the rib eye pieces and stir until evenly coated. Cover and refrigerate for at least 2 hours or overnight.

Preheat smoker and add wood following the manufacturer's instructions. Heat to 225 degrees F and grease a metal baking sheet.

Drain the steak bites from the marinade and spread on the prepared baking sheet. Place in smoker, close lid, and cook until the internal temperature reaches about 135 degrees F, about 1 1/2 hours, turning over once halfway through cooking time.

Remove from the smoker and drizzle with the melted butter, stirring to coat the steak bites. Cool for 10 minutes, stir again, and scoop on a serving platter. Sprinkle with chopped parsley and serve with Horseradish Cream.

Smoked Bacon-Stuffed Mushrooms

MAKES 18 APPETIZERS

18	medium button mushrooms, cleaned
6 strips	regular-sliced bacon
1/3 cup	finely chopped onion
3 tablespoons	mayonnaise
1/2 cup	grated Parmesan cheese
2 tablespoons	freshly chopped parsley, plus more for garnish

Preheat smoker and add wood following the manufacturer's instructions. Heat to 350 degrees F and grease a metal baking sheet.

Remove stems from mushrooms and finely chop the stems, reserving the caps. In a medium skillet, cook bacon until crisp. Remove bacon, drain, and crumble finely. Discard all but 2 tablespoons drippings from skillet. Add chopped mushroom stems and onion, and cook until tender, 5 to 6 minutes. Cool for 5 minutes.

In a small bowl, combine bacon, mushroom-onion mixture, mayonnaise, Parmesan cheese, and chopped parsley. Arrange mushroom caps on prepared baking sheet and fill with bacon mixture. Place baking sheet in the smoker, close the lid, and cook until mushrooms are hot and cheese is melting, about 20 minutes.

Pulled Pork BBQ Nachos

MAKES 4 SERVINGS

1 bag (12 ounces)	restaurant-style corn tortilla chips
2 cups	Simple Pulled Pork (page 93), finely shredded
1/3 cup	barbecue sauce
1/2 cup	shredded Mexican blend cheese
2	large jalapeños, seeded and finely diced
	guacamole, salsa, and sour cream for dipping

Preheat smoker and add wood following the manufacturer's instructions. Heat to 350 degrees F and line a baking sheet with aluminum foil. Spray lightly with nonstick cooking spray.

Spread the tortilla chips in an even layer on the prepared baking sheet. Top with pulled pork and drizzle with barbecue sauce. Sprinkle with cheese. Place the baking sheet in the smoker, close the lid, and cook until cheese is melted and nachos are hot, about 20 minutes.

Remove from smoker, cool for 5 minutes, and sprinkle evenly with chopped jalapeños. Serve with guacamole, salsa, and sour cream for toppings.

#47

Burnt End–Style Franks

MAKES 12 SERVINGS

12	all-beef hot dogs
2 tablespoons	yellow mustard
2 tablespoons	ketchup
¼ cup	All-Around Rub (page 12) or your favorite rub
½ cup	barbecue sauce
1 cup	packed brown sugar

Preheat smoker and add wood following the manufacturer's instructions. Heat to 225 degrees F and grease a 9 x 13-inch metal baking pan.

Arrange hot dogs in the pan, place in the smoker, and close the lid. Cook for 30 minutes. Remove pan, cool for 10 minutes, and cut the hot dogs into 1-inch pieces. Return to the pan and add mustard and ketchup, stirring to coat. Sprinkle all over with the rub, stirring to coat. Place the pan in smoker, close the lid, and cook for another 30 minutes.

Remove from smoker and drizzle with barbecue sauce. Sprinkle with brown sugar and stir until pieces are coated. Return pan to smoker and continue cooking, stirring occasionally, until hot dogs are dark brown and sticky, 30 to 45 minutes. Remove pan from smoker, cool for 10 minutes, and transfer to a serving platter.

Roasted Garlic Parmesan Bread
MAKES 6 SERVINGS

1	head garlic
2 teaspoons	extra virgin olive oil
1/2 cup	salted butter, softened
2 tablespoons	chopped flat-leaf parsley
1	loaf French bread, cut in half horizontally
2 tablespoons	shredded Parmesan cheese

Preheat smoker and add wood following the manufacturer's instructions. Heat to 225 degrees F.

Using a sharp knife, trim off the top of the head of garlic to expose just the tops of the garlic cloves. Place in the center of a 12 x 12-inch piece of heavy-duty aluminum foil and press the foil around the garlic head, leaving the cut top exposed. Drizzle with olive oil.

Put the foil-enclosed garlic on the smoker rack, close the lid, and cook until cloves are tender and golden brown, about 1 1/2 hours. Remove, cool for 10 minutes, and squeeze the garlic cloves into a medium bowl. Add the butter and mash with a fork until combined. Add the parsley and stir with a fork to combine.

Spread the garlic butter mixture across both halves of the bread loaf and put on the prepared baking sheet, cut side up. Place in the smoker, close the lid, and cook for 15 minutes. Sprinkle with the Parmesan cheese and continue cooking until bread is crispy and golden brown, 10 to 15 more minutes. Cool for 5 minutes and cut into slices with a serrated knife.

Smoked Bacon and Cheese Potato Skins

MAKES 12 SERVINGS

6	medium russet potatoes (about 3 pounds)
	vegetable oil
	salt
	freshly ground pepper
12 strips	bacon, fried and crumbled
1 cup	shredded cheddar cheese
2	green onions, thinly sliced
	sour cream for dipping

Preheat smoker and add wood following the manufacturer's instructions. Heat to 200 degrees F. Poke the potatoes in several places with a fork, and arrange them on the grill grate over indirect heat. Cook for 30 minutes. Increase the heat to 400 degrees F. Turn potatoes over and continue cooking until tender, 40 to 50 minutes. Remove and cool.

Cut potatoes in half horizontally, and use a spoon to carefully scoop out the insides, leaving a shell about 1/4 inch thick. (Save scooped-out potatoes for another use.) Cut each shell in half lengthwise.

Increase the smoker temperature to 450 degrees F. Brush potato skins with vegetable oil and sprinkle with salt and pepper. Arrange on a baking sheet, put in the smoker, and cook for 10 minutes; turn over and continue cooking until potato skins are golden brown and crispy, about 10 to 15 more minutes. Sprinkle with bacon and cheese and return to smoker. Cook until cheese is melted, about 5 minutes. Top with green onions and serve with sour cream.

Bacon-Jalapeño Poppers
MAKES 12 SERVINGS

8 ounces	**cream cheese, softened**
¼ teaspoon	**garlic powder**
¼ teaspoon	**salt**
¼ teaspoon	**freshly ground black pepper**
2 tablespoons	**finely chopped green onions**
½ cup	**shredded sharp cheddar cheese**
½ cup	**shredded Monterey Jack cheese**
½ pound	**regular sliced smoked bacon, cooked and crumbled**
12	**medium jalapeños, cut in half lengthwise, seeds removed**
	chopped cilantro, for garnish

Preheat smoker and add wood following the manufacturer's instructions. Heat to 225 degrees F and line a baking sheet with aluminum foil.

In a medium bowl, combine cream cheese, garlic powder, salt, pepper, green onions, cheddar cheese, Monterey Jack cheese, and crumbled bacon. Remove the ribs from the inside of the jalapeños with a spoon and fill generously with cream cheese mixture. Arrange, cut side up, on prepared baking sheet and place on the smoker grill grates. Close the lid and cook until hot and bubbling, about 1 hour. Garnish with chopped cilantro before serving, if desired.

Sweet and Spicy Bacon-Wrapped Meatballs

MAKES 12 SERVINGS

1 pound	regular-sliced smoked bacon
24	frozen and thawed or fresh fully cooked 1¹/₂-inch meatballs
2 tablespoons	All-Around Rub (page 12) or your favorite rub
³/₄ cup	hot pepper jelly

Preheat smoker and add wood following the manufacturer's instructions. Heat to 225 degrees F and line a baking sheet with aluminum foil.

Cut bacon slices in half widthwise. Lay 1 meatball on each half-slice and roll the bacon around the meatball, securing with a toothpick. Arrange bacon-wrapped meatballs on prepared baking sheet and sprinkle with rub.

Place baking sheet in the smoker, close the lid, and cook for 45 minutes. Turn meatballs over, blot bacon grease with paper towels, and continue cooking until bacon is brown and crispy, about 45 more minutes.

Heat the pepper jelly in a small saucepan over medium heat and stir until melted. Brush the meatballs all over with the melted jelly. Return to the smoker and cook until sauce is hot and sticky, about 15 more minutes. Cool for 10 minutes and serve.

Sticky-Sweet Pork Belly Burnt Ends

MAKES 12 SERVINGS

1	center-cut piece pork belly, about 4 pounds and 1 to 1$^1/_4$ inches thick*
$^1/_4$ cup	All-Around Rub (page 12) or your favorite rub
$^1/_3$ cup	packed brown sugar
1$^2/_3$ cups	Smokin' Good BBQ Sauce (page 20) or your favorite barbecue sauce

Preheat smoker and add wood following the manufacturer's instructions. Heat to 275 degrees F.

Remove the skin and trim pork belly, if necessary, so fat cap is about $^1/_2$ inch. Sprinkle all over with the rub, using fingers to rub into the meat. Place pork belly, fat side up, directly on the smoker grill grate, close lid, and cook until the internal temperature reaches 180 degrees F, about 3$^1/_2$ to 4 hours. Carefully remove the pork belly and wrap it in aluminum foil.

Place it back into the smoker, close lid, and cook until the internal temperature reaches 200 degrees F, 80 to 90 minutes.

In a small saucepan, add the brown sugar to the barbecue sauce and stir until combined. Cook over medium heat for 5 minutes and set aside.

Remove pork belly from foil, transfer to cutting board, and use a sharp knife to cut in 1$^1/_2$-inch cubes. Spread cubes in 9 x 13-inch metal or disposable aluminum pan, and pour warm sauce over the top, making sure all pieces are well coated. Cover the pan with foil, and place into the smoker for 30 minutes. Remove foil, return to smoker, and cook until sauce reduces slightly and gets dark and sticky, 30 to 40 more minutes. Cool for 15 minutes, and serve.

*A center-cut slab of pork belly with an even meat-to-fat ratio will yield the best result.

#53

Smoked Almonds

MAKES 8 SERVINGS

2 cups	**blanched, peeled whole almonds**
1 tablespoon	**butter, melted**
1 tablespoon	**bacon grease**
2 teaspoons	**kosher salt**

Preheat smoker and add wood following the manufacturer's instructions. Heat to 220 degrees F.

Add almonds to a rimmed metal baking sheet and place it in the smoker. Close the lid and smoke the almonds until lightly browned and smoky, about 1^1/$_2$ hours, stirring at the 45-minute mark. Remove from smoker and cool for 5 minutes.

Add the butter and bacon grease to the baking pan and stir well to coat the almonds. Sprinkle with kosher salt and return the pan to the smoker until almonds are golden brown, about 30 minutes. Remove and cool for 10 minutes.

Smoky Snack Mix

MAKES 12 SERVINGS

1 cup	butter, melted
2	garlic cloves, peeled and minced
2 tablespoons	Worcestershire sauce
1¼ teaspoons	seasoned salt
¼ teaspoon	freshly ground black pepper
3 cups	Corn Chex cereal
2 cups	Wheat Chex cereal
1½ cups	potato stick snacks
1½ cups	Bugle corn snacks, broken in half
1 cup	rye chips
1 cup	honey-mustard pretzel chunks
1 cup	cheese-flavored baby Goldfish crackers
1 cup	shelled, roasted pistachio nuts

Preheat smoker and add wood following the manufacturer's instructions. Heat to 275 degrees F.

Combine the butter, garlic, Worcestershire sauce, seasoned salt, and pepper in a large bowl. Add the cereals, potato sticks, Bugles, rye chips, pretzel chunks, Goldfish, and nuts and stir until all pieces are coated.

Spoon onto 2 rimmed baking sheets and cook in the smoker until crispy, about 1 hour and 30 minutes, stirring every 20 minutes. Cool for 10 minutes before serving.

Smoked Olives

MAKES 8 SERVINGS

2 cups	**assorted olives, drained**
2 tablespoons	**extra virgin olive oil**
1	**garlic clove, minced**
$1/2$ teaspoon	**dried oregano**
$1/4$ teaspoon	**freshly ground black pepper**
2 tablespoons	**shredded Parmesan cheese**

Preheat smoker and add wood following the manufacturer's instructions. Heat to 220 degrees F.

In a medium bowl, combine the olives, olive oil, garlic, oregano, and pepper and stir. Spread the mixture in an 8 x 8-inch metal baking dish. Place in the smoker, close the lid, and cook for 30 minutes. Stir and smoke for 10 more minutes.

Remove from the smoker and cool to room temperature. Transfer to a serving dish, sprinkle with the Parmesan cheese, stir to coat, and serve.

#56–70

SIDES
&
SALADS

#56

Smoked Mashed Potatoes

MAKES 6 SERVINGS

2 pounds	russet potatoes, peeled and quartered
9 tablespoons	butter, cut into $1/2$-inch slices, divided
1	medium sweet yellow onion, such as Vidalia, finely chopped
$1/3$ cup	cream cheese, cut into 1-inch cubes
1 cup	half-and-half, warmed, divided
1 teaspoon	salt, plus more to taste
2	garlic cloves, minced

Put potatoes in a large pot and cover with cold water to cover by 1 inch. Bring to a boil over high heat. Reduce heat to a simmer and cook until potatoes are fork-tender, 20 to 25 minutes.

While the potatoes are cooking, heat 1 tablespoon butter in a small skillet over medium-low heat. Add the onion and cook, stirring occasionally, until translucent, about 5 minutes. Add the cubed cream cheese and stir until cream cheese melts. Cover and set aside.

Preheat smoker and add wood following the manufacturer's instructions. Heat to 225 degrees F. Grease a 12-inch cast iron skillet.

Drain potatoes in a colander and shake a few times to remove all the liquid so the potatoes are very dry. Return to the pot, add the remaining sliced butter, and lightly mash with a potato masher until the butter is all melted and incorporated. Add $7/8$ cup of the half-and-half, salt, and garlic and continue mashing. Add the onion mixture and continue mashing. Add the remaining half-and-half if needed to make a smooth, creamy mixture. Spread the mashed potatoes in the prepared skillet, place in the smoker, and close the lid. Smoke until potatoes are hot and bubbling, about 1 hour.

#57

Smoked Corn on the Cob with Garlic Chive Butter

MAKES 6 SERVINGS

6 tablespoons	**unsalted butter, melted**
2	**garlic cloves, minced**
¹/₄ teaspoon	**salt**
¹/₄ teaspoon	**freshly ground black pepper**
6 ears	**sweet corn, shucked**
2 teaspoons	**chopped fresh chives**

Preheat smoker and add wood following the manufacturer's instructions. Heat to 225 degrees F. In a small bowl, combine the butter, garlic, salt, and pepper. Brush about half of the mixture all over the ears of corn.

Arrange the corn directly on the smoker grates, close the lid, and smoke for 20 minutes. Brush the corn with the butter mixture again, turn over and brush the other side. Continue cooking until corn is tender, 15 to 20 more minutes. Sprinkle with chopped chives and serve.

Buttery Parmesan Cauliflower

MAKES 6 SERVINGS

1	medium head cauliflower, leaves removed
2 tablespoons	extra virgin olive oil
2 tablespoons	butter, melted
2	garlic cloves, minced
1 tablespoon	All-Around Rub (page 12) or your favorite rub
$1/2$	fresh lemon
$1/4$ cup	grated Parmesan cheese

Preheat smoker and add wood following the manufacturer's instructions. Heat to 375 degrees F. Using a sharp knife, cut the stem off the cauliflower even with the head so the head can sit upright.

In a small bowl, combine the olive oil, butter, and garlic. Brush the mixture all over the cauliflower to coat. Sprinkle with the rub. Place the cauliflower directly on the grill grate, close the lid, and cook until tender and a knife inserts easily, 60 to 75 minutes.

Remove cauliflower to a cutting board, cool for 10 minutes, and cut in slices or florets. Squeeze fresh lemon on top and sprinkle with Parmesan cheese.

Glazed Smoky Yams

MAKES 6 SERVINGS

2 pounds	**yams, peeled and cut lengthwise into 1½-inch wedges**
2 tablespoons	**olive oil**
¼ cup	**sugar**
1 tablespoon	**cinnamon**
½ teaspoon	**salt**
⅛ teaspoon	**ground ginger**

Preheat smoker and add wood following the manufacturer's instructions. Heat to 275 degrees F. Grease a metal baking sheet. Place the yam wedges in a large bowl and drizzle with the olive oil, stirring to coat.

In a small bowl, whisk together the sugar, cinnamon, salt, and ginger until blended. Remove 1 tablespoon of the mixture to a separate dish and set aside. Sprinkle the rest of the mixture over the yam wedges and stir to coat.

Spread yams in prepared baking sheet and place in the smoker. Close the lid and cook for 30 minutes. Stir and continue cooking until potatoes are fork-tender, 30 to 45 more minutes. Remove from the smoker, cool for 5 minutes, and sprinkle all over with the remaining sugar mixture. Serve hot.

Smoked Green Beans with Parmesan Cheese

MAKES 6 SERVINGS

1½ pounds	fresh green beans, washed and trimmed
½ cup	salted butter, melted
1	garlic clove, minced
½ teaspoon	salt
¼ teaspoon	freshly ground black pepper
½ cup	shredded Parmesan cheese

Preheat smoker and add wood following the manufacturer's instructions. Heat to 225 degrees F.

Bring a large pot of water to a boil over medium-high heat. Add the beans and cook for 3 minutes. Drain and transfer to a large bowl. Pour in the melted butter, garlic, salt, and pepper, and toss until evenly coated. Transfer to a 9 x 13-inch metal baking pan.

Place the pan in the smoker, close the lid, and smoke for 30 minutes. Stir with a large spoon and continue cooking until beans are tender, about 30 more minutes.

Remove from smoker, cool for 5 minutes, and sprinkle with Parmesan cheese.

Smokehouse Brussels Sprouts

MAKES 8 SERVINGS

1¹/₂ pounds	Brussels sprouts, trimmed and halved
1 tablespoon	extra virgin olive oil
1 teaspoon	salt
1 teaspoon	freshly ground black pepper
2 tablespoons	balsamic vinegar
2 tablespoons	honey
6 strips	thick-sliced smoked bacon, cooked and crumbled

Preheat smoker and add wood following the manufacturer's instructions. Heat to 225 degrees F.

Spread the Brussels sprouts in a 9 x 13-inch metal baking pan. Drizzle with olive oil and stir to coat. Sprinkle with salt and pepper, stirring to coat. Place the pan, uncovered, in the smoker and cook until sprouts are fork-tender, 75 to 90 minutes.

In a small dish, whisk together the vinegar and honey until smooth. Drizzle over sprouts and stir to coat. Add the crumbled bacon and stir to combine. Smoke for 10 more minutes. Remove from smoker, cool for 10 minutes, and serve.

Toasty Marshmallow Sweet Potatoes

MAKES 6 SERVINGS

6	medium sweet potatoes, scrubbed
2 tablespoons	extra virgin olive oil
1 tablespoon	kosher salt
$^1/_2$ cup	butter, softened
$^1/_3$ cup	packed brown sugar
1 teaspoon	cinnamon
$^1/_4$ teaspoon	salt
$1^1/_2$ cups	mini marshmallows

Preheat smoker and add wood following the manufacturer's instructions. Heat to 225 degrees F.

Poke the potatoes with a fork several times and brush all over with olive oil. Sprinkle with kosher salt and arrange directly on smoker rack. Close lid and cook until fork-tender, $1^1/_2$ to 2 hours, turning over once halfway through cooking.

Remove potatoes from the smoker and place them onto a large cutting board. Increase the heat and temperature of the smoker to 475 degrees F.

In a small bowl, combine softened butter with brown sugar, cinnamon, and salt and stir to blend. Cut a slit down the middle of each sweet potato. Divide the butter mixture among the potatoes and use a fork to incorporate the baked potato flesh until mixed. Top potatoes with mini marshmallows, pressing gently to adhere, and arrange potatoes on a metal baking sheet. Place in the smoker directly on the grill grates. Close the lid and cook until marshmallows are lightly toasted, 5 to 7 minutes. Remove from smoker and cool for 10 minutes before serving.

Smoked Twice-Baked Potatoes

MAKES 8 SERVINGS

4	large russet potatoes
1/2 cup	milk, warmed
6 tablespoons	butter, melted
1/2 cup	sour cream
1 tablespoon	minced green onion, plus extra for garnish
4 strips	thick-sliced smoked bacon, cooked and drained
1 cup	shredded sharp cheddar cheese, divided
1/2 teaspoon	salt
1/2 teaspoon	freshly ground black pepper

Preheat smoker and add wood following the manufacturer's instructions. Heat to 400 degrees F. Wash and dry the potatoes and prick in several places with a fork. Arrange directly on the grill grates, close lid, and cook until potatoes are cooked through, turning over once halfway during cooking, 60 to 75 minutes. Cool for 10 minutes.

Reduce the smoker temperature to 375 degrees F and grease a metal baking sheet.

Cut the potatoes in half lengthwise and scoop the potato flesh into a large bowl, leaving a 1/4-inch-thick layer of flesh in the potato skins. Mash the potatoes with the milk and melted butter until mostly smooth. Stir in the sour cream, green onion, bacon, half of the cheese, salt, and pepper. Spoon the filling into the potato shells and sprinkle with remaining cheese. Arrange on prepared baking sheet and put it in the smoker. Close the lid and cook until the potatoes are hot and cheese is melted, 25 to 30 minutes. Remove from smoker, cool for 10 minutes, and garnish with green onions.

Maple-Pecan Butternut Squash

MAKES 8 TO 10 SERVINGS

3 pounds	butternut squash, peeled, seeded, and cut into 1-inch cubes
2 tablespoons	extra virgin olive oil
2 tablespoons	maple syrup
1/2 teaspoon	cinnamon
1/2 teaspoon	salt
1/2 teaspoon	freshly ground black pepper
1/4 cup	packed brown sugar
1 tablespoon	water
1 cup	pecan halves, roughly chopped

Preheat smoker and add wood following the manufacturer's instructions. Heat to 400 degrees F. Grease a 9 x 13-inch metal baking pan, and line a baking sheet with parchment paper.

Spread the squash in the prepared baking pan and drizzle with the olive oil and maple syrup, stirring to coat. Sprinkle with the cinnamon, salt, and pepper, and stir to coat. Put the pan in the smoker, close the lid, and cook until squash is tender, 45 to 60 minutes, stirring occasionally.

Meanwhile, combine the brown sugar and water in a nonstick skillet over medium-high heat and cook until mixture bubbles, about 3 minutes. Add pecans and cook, stirring frequently, until pecans are fragrant and most of the liquid evaporates, 3 to 4 minutes. Spread pecans in a single layer on the parchment-lined baking sheet, and use a fork to separate. Cool to room temperature.

When squash is done, remove pan from smoker, cool for 10 minutes, and top with sugared pecans.

Smoked Bacon Deviled Eggs

MAKES 12 SERVINGS

12	hard-boiled eggs, peeled
1/2 cup	mayonnaise
1 1/2 teaspoons	yellow mustard
1/2 teaspoon	curry powder (optional)
1/4 teaspoon	salt
1/4 teaspoon	freshly ground black pepper
6 slices	thick-sliced smoked bacon, cooked and drained, divided smoked paprika for sprinkling

Preheat smoker and add wood following the manufacturer's instructions. Heat to 175 degrees F.

Place the peeled hard-boiled eggs on the grill grates over indirect heat and smoke for 30 minutes. Remove from the smoker and cool in the refrigerator for 2 hours.

Cut smoked eggs down the middle and put yolks in a medium bowl. Mash yolks with a fork, then stir in mayonnaise, mustard, curry powder, salt, and pepper until well blended. Chop 4 bacon slices finely and add to the yolk mixture, stirring well to blend. Cut each of the remaining 2 bacon slices into 6 squares each for garnish.

Spoon or pipe about 1 tablespoon yolk mixture into the hollow of each egg white. Garnish each egg with a bacon square. Sprinkle the tops with smoked paprika.

Smoky Baked Beans with Bacon

MAKES 6 SERVINGS

1 pound	thick-sliced smoked bacon, chopped
1	medium onion, diced
2	large jalapeños, seeded and diced
2	garlic cloves, minced
3 cans (15 ounces each)	baked beans
$^1/_2$ cup	barbecue sauce
$^1/_2$ cup	packed brown sugar
$^1/_2$ cup	beer (or substitute beef broth)
2 tablespoons	molasses
2 tablespoons	ketchup
1 tablespoon	Dijon mustard
1 tablespoon	Worcestershire sauce
	salt and freshly ground black pepper, to taste

Preheat smoker and add wood following the manufacturer's instructions. Heat to 225 degrees F.

In a large cast iron skillet, cook the bacon over medium heat on the stovetop until brown and crispy. Use a slotted spoon to transfer bacon to paper towels to drain. Pour out all but 1 tablespoon drippings. Add the onion and cook over medium heat until translucent, about 5 minutes. Add the jalapeños and garlic and cook for 1 more minute. Add the beans, barbecue sauce, brown sugar, beer, molasses, ketchup, mustard, Worcestershire sauce, and bacon. Stir until thoroughly combined.

Place the skillet in the smoker, close the lid, and smoke until beans are hot and bubbling, 2 to $2^1/_2$ hours. Stir the beans every 30 minutes, adding water if they become dry. Cool for 10 minutes and add salt and pepper to taste.

Smoked Turkey Salad

MAKES 6 SERVINGS

³/₄ cup	pecan halves, chopped
¹/₃ cup	extra virgin olive oil
2 tablespoons	balsamic vinegar
1 teaspoon	Dijon mustard
³/₄ teaspoon	salt
¹/₄ teaspoon	freshly ground black pepper
1 pound	chilled Easy Smoked Turkey Breast (page 100) or thick-sliced deli smoked turkey, chopped into ¹/₂-inch cubes
1 pound	baby spinach, stems removed
¹/₄ pound	thick-sliced smoked bacon, cooked and crumbled
4 ounces	Cambozola or Gorgonzola cheese, cut into ¹/₂-inch cubes
1	large Granny Smith apple, peeled, cored, and cut into ¹/₂-inch matchstick pieces

Preheat smoker and add wood following the manufacturer's instructions. Heat to 225 degrees F and line a rimmed metal baking sheet with aluminum foil.

Spread the pecans on prepared baking sheet and place in the smoker. Close the lid and cook until pecans are fragrant and lightly toasted, about 30 minutes. Cool and set aside.

In a small glass jar, combine the olive oil, vinegar, mustard, salt, and pepper and shake until mixture is blended.

Place the turkey in a large bowl and drizzle with half of the dressing, stirring with a fork to coat. Add the spinach, pecans, bacon, cheese, and apple. Drizzle with the remaining dressing, toss and serve.

Smoked Italian Pasta Salad

MAKES 8 TO 10 SERVINGS

1/2	medium red onion, chopped
1 pound	hard salami, cut into 1/3-inch cubes
1	green bell pepper, seeded and diced
3 cups	grape tomatoes, halved
1/3 cup	sliced black olives
1/3 cup	sliced pimiento-stuffed green olives
1/3 cup	sliced pepperoncini peppers
1 pound	dry rotini or fusilli (corkscrew) pasta
2/3 cup	Italian salad dressing, divided
1/2 pound	cherry-size *Ciliegine* mozzarella balls, halved
	salt and freshly ground black pepper to taste
1/4 cup	chopped parsley

In a small bowl of ice water, soak the red onion for 10 minutes to crisp and mellow. Drain and set aside.

Preheat smoker and add wood following the manufacturer's instructions. Heat to 180 degrees F.

On a metal baking sheet, spread the salami, bell pepper, tomatoes, black and green olives, and pepperoncini in a single layer. Place the tray directly on the smoker grill grates. Close the lid and smoke for 15 minutes. Remove and cool.

Meanwhile, bring a large pot of salted water to a boil. Add the pasta and cook according to package instructions. Drain the pasta and transfer to a large bowl. Drizzle with half the Italian dressing, stir to mix, and cool for 10 minutes. Add the smoked salami, pepper, tomatoes, olives, pepperoncini, red onion, and mozzarella balls. Drizzle with the remaining Italian dressing and toss well to coat. Season with salt and pepper. Cover and refrigerate for at least 1 hour, and up to overnight. Garnish with chopped parsley just before serving.

#69
14K Bacon-Wrapped Carrots
MAKES 8 SERVINGS

3 pounds	**whole medium carrots, peeled**
1¹/₂ pounds	**regular-sliced smoked bacon**
	salt and freshly ground black pepper for sprinkling
¹/₂ cup	**maple syrup**

Preheat smoker and add wood following the manufacturer's instructions. Heat to 400 degrees F and line a rimmed metal baking sheet with aluminum foil.

Wrap each carrot in a slice of bacon, stretching to cover, and overlapping the ends so they are secured. Sprinkle each carrot with salt and pepper.

Arrange the carrots on the prepared baking sheet and place in the smoker. Close lid and cook for 15 minutes. Turn carrots over, blot excess grease with paper towels, and brush with maple syrup. Cook for 10 more minutes, turn over carrots, blot excess grease, and brush with maple syrup. Cook until bacon is brown and crispy, 5 to 10 more minutes. Remove from smoker, cool for 10 minutes, blot excess grease, and serve.

Roasted Red Potato Salad with Bacon

MAKES 8 SERVINGS

3 pounds	small new potatoes, quartered
2	shallots, chopped
2 tablespoons	melted butter
1 cup	sour cream
$^2/_3$ cup	mayonnaise
1 tablespoon	chopped chives, plus extra for garnish
$^1/_4$ teaspoon	salt
$^1/_4$ teaspoon	freshly ground black pepper
$^1/_2$ cup	chopped celery
12 slices	bacon, cooked and crumbled

Preheat smoker and add wood following the manufacturer's instructions. Heat to 275 degrees F.

Place the potatoes and shallots in a large bowl, drizzle with melted butter, and stir to coat. Spread the potatoes in a 9 x 13-inch metal baking pan. Place the pan in the smoker, close the lid, and smoke, stirring every 30 minutes, until potatoes are fork tender, 1 to $1^1/_2$ hours. Cool for 10 minutes.

In a large bowl, combine the sour cream, mayonnaise, chives, salt, and pepper. Add the warm potatoes and celery, and stir to combine. Cool the salad to room temperature, then chill overnight. Before serving, stir in crumbled bacon and garnish with chopped chives.

MAIN COURSES

Smoked Prime Rib with Horseradish Cream

MAKES 6 SERVINGS

1	lean end (6 pounds) 3-bone prime rib, excess fat trimmed
1/2 cup	stone-ground mustard
2 tablespoons	Worcestershire sauce
4	garlic cloves, minced
	kosher salt and freshly ground black pepper for sprinkling
	Horseradish Cream (page 24)

One hour before cooking, remove the prime rib from the refrigerator and bring to room temperature. Preheat smoker and add wood following the manufacturer's instructions. Heat to 250 degrees F.

In a small bowl, combine the mustard, Worcestershire sauce, and garlic. Spread the mixture evenly over the prime rib and season liberally with salt and pepper.

Place the roast on the grill grates, insert a probe thermometer, and close the lid. Smoke until the internal temperature reaches 120 to 125 degrees F for rare or 130 to 135 degrees F for medium. Cooking time for medium rare is approximately 3 to 3 1/2 hours, but exact time will vary depending on size and thickness of roast. The meat will continue cooking as it rests.

Remove the roast from the smoker and transfer to a rimmed baking sheet. Tent loosely with aluminum foil and allow to rest for 20 minutes before slicing. Serve with Horseradish Cream.

Easy Homemade Pastrami

MAKES 8 SERVINGS

1	brined flat-cut corned beef, about 4 pounds
2 tablespoons	stone-ground mustard
1 tablespoon	freshly ground black pepper
2 teaspoons	ground coriander
2 teaspoons	brown sugar
$1/2$ teaspoon	smoked paprika
$1/2$ teaspoon	garlic powder
$1/4$ teaspoon	onion powder

Remove the corned beef from the packaging, drain and discard liquid, and rinse under cool water. Trim off excess fat. Transfer to a pot and cover with cold water. Refrigerate for 1 hour. Drain water, refill to cover beef, and refrigerate for 1 more hour. Drain the water and pat dry.

Preheat smoker and add wood following the manufacturer's directions. Heat to 225 degrees F.

Spread the mustard on all sides of the corned beef. Whisk together the pepper, coriander, brown sugar, paprika, garlic powder, and onion powder in a small bowl. Sprinkle the mixture all over the corned beef, pressing to adhere to surface. Place brisket directly on smoker grill grates, close lid, and cook until internal temperature reaches 160 degrees F, $5 1/2$ to 6 hours.

Remove beef from smoker and wrap in a double layer of aluminum foil. Return to smoker, increase temperature to 325 degrees F, and cook until internal temperature reaches 200 degrees F, about 2 more hours. Remove from smoker and rest for 1 hour. Unwrap and slice thinly across the grain.

Smoky Cheddar Meatloaf

MAKES 6 SERVINGS

1¹/₂ pounds	**ground beef**
1 cup	**seasoned breadcrumbs**
¹/₃ cup	**ketchup**
2	**eggs, lightly beaten**
1 tablespoon	**yellow mustard**
2 teaspoons	**Worcestershire sauce**
1¹/₄ teaspoons	**salt**
1 teaspoon	**freshly ground black pepper**
2 cups	**shredded sharp cheddar cheese**

Preheat smoker and add wood following the manufacturer's instructions. Heat to 350 degrees F. Grease a 9 x 5-inch metal loaf pan.

In a large bowl, combine the ground beef, breadcrumbs, ketchup, eggs, mustard, Worcestershire sauce, salt, and pepper.

Spread half of the meatloaf mixture in the bottom of the loaf pan. Sprinkle evenly with the cheese and spread with the remaining meatloaf mixture.

Set the loaf pan on a baking sheet to catch drips and place in the smoker. Close the lid and smoke until a thermometer reads 165 degrees F, 60 to 75 minutes. Remove from the smoker, cool for 15 minutes, and cut into slices to serve.

Smoked Beef Short Ribs

MAKES 4 SERVINGS

2 tablespoons	**stone-ground mustard**
4	**garlic cloves, minced**
2 pounds	**beef short ribs, silver skin and excess fat removed**
2 teaspoons	**kosher salt**
2 teaspoons	**freshly ground black pepper**
²/₃ cup	**beef stock or broth**

Preheat smoker and add wood following the manufacturer's instructions. Heat to 225 degrees F. In a small dish, stir together the mustard and garlic and spread over the ribs. Sprinkle all over with salt and pepper.

Place the ribs directly on the smoker grill grates and insert a temperature probe parallel to, but not touching, a bone. Close the lid and smoke for 3 hours.

Meanwhile, pour the beef stock into a food-safe spray bottle. After 3 hours, spray ribs generously with beef stock. Continue cooking, spray-basting with stock every hour, until the internal temperature reads 200 to 205 degrees F, 6 to 7 hours total cooking time.

Remove ribs from smoker, place in a 9 x 13-inch metal or disposable aluminum pan, and cover loosely with aluminum foil. Let ribs rest for 1 hour before serving.

Cowpoke Beef Stew

MAKES 8 SERVINGS

2¹/₂ pounds	beef chuck roast, cut into 1¹/₂-inch cubes
3 tablespoons	flour
1 teaspoon	salt
1 teaspoon	freshly ground black pepper
1 tablespoon	vegetable oil
1 tablespoon	butter
3¹/₂ cups	beef stock or broth
1	large onion, chopped
4	garlic cloves, minced
1 tablespoon	tomato paste
1 tablespoon	Worcestershire sauce
1¹/₂ teaspoons	dried oregano
3	large carrots, cut into ¹/₂-inch pieces
3	medium Yukon Gold potatoes, cut into 1-inch cubes
³/₄ cup	fresh or frozen and thawed green peas
	chopped flat-leaf parsley, for garnish

Preheat smoker and add wood following the manufacturer's instructions. Heat to 300 degrees F.

Place the chuck roast cubes in a large bowl, sprinkle with flour, salt, and pepper, and toss to coat. Heat the oil and butter in a large Dutch oven over medium heat and brown the beef cubes in batches; transfer to a plate and set aside. Add the beef stock to the Dutch oven, scraping the browned bits. Stir in the onion, garlic, tomato paste, Worcestershire sauce, oregano, and the beef cubes. Place the Dutch oven, uncovered, in smoker, close the lid, and cook for 2 hours, stirring every 30 minutes. Add the carrots and potatoes, cover pot, and continue cooking for $1\frac{1}{2}$ hours. Add peas and continue cooking until vegetables are tender, about 30 more minutes. Remove from smoker, cool for 10 minutes, and garnish with chopped parsley.

#76

Simple Pulled Pork

MAKES 10 TO 12 SERVINGS

1	**fresh pork butt roast (6$\frac{1}{2}$ to 7 pounds)**
5 cups	**Pork Brine (page 19)**
3 tablespoons	**Ancho Chili Garlic Rub (page 14) or your favorite sweet rub**
	barbecue sauce

Place the pork butt in a food-safe brining container and pour in the brine. Cover and refrigerate for at least 4 hours or overnight. After brining is complete, remove the pork butt and pat dry with paper towels.

Preheat smoker and add wood following the manufacturer's instructions. Heat to 225 degrees F. Apply the rub all over the pork butt, patting to adhere. Place a roasting rack in a drip pan and transfer the pork butt to the rack. Place in the smoker and cook until internal temperature reaches 202 degrees F, $9\frac{1}{2}$ to $10\frac{1}{2}$ hours. Remove from smoker, tent with aluminum foil, and rest for 15 minutes. Use 2 forks to shred meat, discarding any fat, and serve with barbecue sauce.

Smoked Pork Tenderloin Wrapped in Bacon

MAKES 4 SERVINGS

1	garlic clove, minced
1	pork tenderloin (1½ pounds), excess fat, silver skin, and membrane removed
2 tablespoons	All-Around Rub (page 12)
½ teaspoon	freshly ground black pepper
6 strips	regular-sliced bacon
1	lime, cut into wedges

Preheat the oven to 350 degrees. Line a baking sheet with aluminum foil and fit it with a wire baking rack.

Rub the minced garlic into the tenderloin. Sprinkle on both sides with the seasoning mixture and black pepper. Allow to sit for 20 minutes to absorb the seasonings.

Meanwhile, spread 6 bacon strips on the wire rack. Bake in the oven for about 10 minutes, until the edges start to curl and some of the bacon fat is rendered. Blot with paper towels.

Preheat smoker and add wood following the manufacturer's instructions. Heat to 225 degrees F.

Wrap tenderloin with the partially cooked bacon strips, leaving about ⅓ inch between strips and tucking the ends underneath. Put the bacon-wrapped tenderloin on the wire rack on the baking sheet. Put in the smoker, close lid, and smoke until the internal temperature measures 143 degrees F, 2½ to 3 hours. Remove from the heat, tent with aluminum foil, and allow to rest for 10 minutes. The pork will continue cooking as it rests to reach an internal temperature of 145 degrees F. Cut the pork tenderloin into slices and serve with lime wedges.

Smoked Cola-Marinated Pork

MAKES 10 SERVINGS

1	boneless pork shoulder (6 to 8 pounds), excess fat trimmed
1	bottle (2-liter) regular cola
1/2 cup	packed brown sugar
1/4 cup	salt
8	garlic cloves, minced
1/2 cup	All-Around Rub (page 12) or your favorite rub
	barbecue sauce

Place the pork in a food-safe brining container with a lid. In a large bowl, combine the cola, brown sugar, salt, and garlic, and stir until sugar and salt dissolve. (Mixture will foam and subside.) Pour over the pork, cover, and refrigerate for 24 hours.

Preheat smoker and add wood following the manufacturer's instructions. Heat to 225 degrees F. Pat pork dry with paper towels. Sprinkle the rub liberally all over the pork, patting to adhere. Place the roast, fat side up, in a 9 x 13-inch metal or disposable aluminum pan. Place the pan in the smoker, close the lid, and smoke for 3 hours. Remove from smoker, wrap in a double layer of aluminum foil, and return to smoker. Continue cooking until a thermometer registers 200 to 205 degrees F, 9 to 13 more hours.

Remove from smoker and let meat cool and rest for 1 hour. Using 2 forks, shred and pull the meat apart, discarding any fat. Serve with barbecue sauce.

Easy Baby Back Ribs

MAKES 4 SERVINGS

2	racks baby back ribs, fat trimmed and membrane removed
⅓ cup	Rib Rub (page 13) or your favorite rub
1 cup	barbecue sauce, plus extra for serving

Rub the ribs all over with the Rib Rub. Cover and refrigerate for 4 to 8 hours.

Remove ribs from refrigerator and let sit at room temperature for 1 hour. Preheat smoker and add wood following the manufacturer's instructions. Heat to 225 degrees F. Place the rib racks on the smoker, meaty side up, and cook for 3 hours. Meanwhile, prepare 2 double sheets of heavy-duty aluminum foil long enough to wrap around each rib rack. Take the ribs off the smoker, place on foil sheets, and brush generously with barbecue sauce. Tightly wrap each rack and return to smoker. Cook until tender, 2 to 3 more hours.

Carefully open foil packets, brush generously with sauce and cook until sauce is sticky, 15 to 20 minutes. Remove from smoker and rest for 15 minutes. Cut between bones and serve with additional barbecue sauce.

Twice-Smoked Maple-Bourbon Ham

MAKES 12 SERVINGS PLUS LEFTOVERS

3 tablespoons	Dijon mustard
1	spiral sliced smoked ham (about 10 pounds)
2 tablespoons	All-Around Rub (page 12) or your favorite rub
1 cup	packed brown sugar
¹⁄₂ cup	maple syrup
¹⁄₄ cup	apple cider vinegar
¹⁄₄ cup	bourbon
¹⁄₄ teaspoon	cayenne pepper

Preheat smoker and add wood following the manufacturer's instructions. Heat to 300 degrees F. Spread the mustard over all surfaces of the ham and sprinkle with the rub, patting to adhere. Place the ham on the smoker grill grates and cook until the internal temperature reaches 120 degrees F, about 3¹⁄₂ hours. Transfer the ham to a metal or disposable aluminum foil roasting pan.

In a small bowl, combine the brown sugar, maple syrup, vinegar, bourbon, and cayenne pepper. Brush the mixture all over the ham, return to smoker, close the lid, and continue cooking, brushing the ham with the glaze every half hour, until the internal temperature reaches 140 degrees F, about 2 more hours. Remove from the smoker and rest 20 minutes before slicing.

Potato, Ham, and Cheese Casserole

MAKES 8 SERVINGS

3 pounds	Yukon gold potatoes, peeled and cut into $1/8$-inch slices
$1/3$ cup	butter
1	small onion, diced
$1/3$ cup	flour
3 cups	milk
$1/2$ cup	chicken stock or broth
	salt and pepper to taste
$1^1/2$ cups	shredded sharp cheddar cheese, divided
2 cups	diced cooked ham

Place the potatoes into a large pot and cover with salted water; bring to a boil. Reduce heat to medium-low and simmer until tender, 10 to 15 minutes. Drain and set aside.

Preheat smoker and add wood following the manufacturer's instructions. Heat to 325 degrees F and grease a 9 x 13-inch metal baking pan.

In a large skillet over medium heat, melt the butter, add onion and cook until tender, about 5 minutes. Sprinkle with flour and cook for 1 minute. Slowly whisk in milk and chicken stock and continue cooking until mixture bubbles and is the consistency of thick cream. Season to taste with salt and pepper.

Arrange half the cooked potatoes in the prepared pan. Sprinkle with 1 cup of the cheese. Spread the ham evenly on top and cover with remaining potatoes. Ladle the sauce evenly over the top and sprinkle with remaining cheese. Place pan in smoker and cook until hot and bubbling, about 60 to 75 minutes.

Smoked Apple Cider Turkey

MAKES 8 SERVINGS

1	whole turkey (about 10 pounds), neck and giblets removed
8 ³/₄ cups	Poultry Brine (page 18)
	olive oil, for brushing
2 tablespoons	All-Around Rub (page 12)
¹/₂ cup	butter
2 cups	apple cider
1	medium Granny Smith apple, quartered
1	medium onion, quartered
4	garlic cloves, chopped
1 tablespoon	salt
1 tablespoon	freshly ground black pepper

Place the turkey in a food-safe brining container and pour in the brine. (Make additional brine if needed so turkey is fully submerged.) Cover and refrigerate for 24 hours. (Note: Skip this step for kosher, enhanced, and self-basting turkeys.) Rinse turkey under cold water and pat dry. Let rest at room temperature for 1 hour.

Preheat smoker and add wood following the manufacturer's instructions. Heat to 225 degrees F. Brush the turkey all over with olive oil and sprinkle the rub all over, patting to adhere. Transfer to a roasting pan. Fill the turkey cavity with butter, apple cider, apple, onion, garlic, salt, and pepper. Cover turkey loosely with aluminum foil. Place the roasting pan in the smoker, close lid, and cook, basting every 1 to 2 hours with juices from the bottom of pan, until turkey is no longer pink at the bone, juices run clear, and an instant-read thermometer inserted in the thickest part of the thigh near the bone reads 180 degrees F, 8 to 10 hours. Remove from smoker and rest for 30 minutes before carving.

Easy Smoked Turkey Breast

MAKES 8 SERVINGS

8 ¾ cups	**Poultry Brine (page 18)**
1	**bone-in turkey breast (about 6 pounds)**
	olive oil, for brushing
3 tablespoons	**All-Around Rub (page 12) or your favorite rub**

Place the turkey breast in a food-safe brining container and pour in the brine. Cover and refrigerate for at least 4 hours or overnight. After brining is complete, rinse the turkey under cold water and pat dry. Let rest at room temperature for 1 hour.

Preheat smoker and add wood following the manufacturer's instructions. Heat to 250 degrees F. Brush the turkey breast all over with the olive oil, and sprinkle generously with the rub. Place directly on the grill grates and cook for 1 hour. Baste with the olive oil and continue cooking until the internal temperature reaches 165 degrees F, 2 to 3 hours.

Remove from the smoker and rest for 10 minutes. Slice thinly across the grain to serve.

Smoked Bacon-Wrapped Chicken

MAKES 6 SERVINGS

¹⁄₂ cup	**All-Around Rub (page 12) or your favorite rub**
12	**chicken thighs, skin removed**
12 strips	**regular-sliced smoked bacon**

Preheat smoker and add wood following the manufacturer's instructions. Heat to 225 degrees F. Line a baking sheet with aluminum foil.

Apply the rub generously all over the chicken thighs. Stretch bacon and wrap 1 strip around each chicken thigh, securing with toothpicks. Sprinkle with more of the rub and pat to adhere.

Arrange on prepared baking sheet and place in the smoker. Cook until bacon starts to brown, 45 minutes to 1 hour. Blot excess grease with paper towels, turn chicken pieces over, tent loosely with aluminum foil, and continue cooking until an instant-read temperature inserted at the thickest part of the chicken reaches 165 degrees F, about 1 more hour. Remove from smoker and cool for 10 minutes.

Beer Can Butter Chicken

MAKES 2 TO 4 SERVINGS

8 3/4 cups	Poultry Brine (page 18)
1	whole chicken (about 4 pounds), giblets removed
2 tablespoons	butter, melted
2 tablespoons	olive oil
1 tablespoon	All-Around Rub (page 12) or your favorite dry rub
1 can (12 ounces)	regular or nonalcoholic beer, room temperature

Pour the brine in a food-safe container and add the chicken, making sure it is completely submerged. Cover the container and refrigerate for 8 to 24 hours. Remove the chicken from the brine, rinse with cool water, and pat dry with paper towels. Let rest at room temperature for 1 hour.

Preheat smoker and add wood following the manufacturer's instructions. Heat to 325 degrees F. In a small dish, combine the butter and olive oil. Rub the mixture on the inside and outside of the entire chicken. Sprinkle inside and out with dry rub, patting to adhere.

Pour out 1/2 can of beer (drink or discard) and place the half-full can on the smoker grill grate. Carefully place the chicken upright on the beer can. Close the lid and cook until internal temperature reaches 165 degrees, about 2 to 2 1/2 hours. Remove from smoker and rest 15 minutes before carving.

Smoked Trout
MAKES 4 SERVINGS

4	small to medium whole trout, cleaned
2	quarts Basic Brine (page 17)
1 tablespoon	kosher salt
2 teaspoons	freshly ground black pepper
4	large fresh dill sprigs
	lemon wedges

Place the trout in a food-safe container and pour in the brine, submerging trout. Cover and refrigerate for 8 hours. Remove trout from brine, rinse under cool water, and pat dry with paper towels. Air dry on a wire rack at room temperature for 1 hour for better smoke absorption.

Preheat smoker and add wood following the manufacturer's instructions. Heat to 180 degrees F.

Season inside and outside of trout with salt and pepper. Place a dill sprig inside each trout.

Place in the smoker, close the lid, and cook until internal temperature reaches 145 degrees F, 3 to 4 hours, turning over once during cooking. Remove trout from smoker and serve warm, or refrigerate, covered, for at least 4 hours, and serve chilled. Accompany with lemon wedges.

Bacon and Green Chile Mac and Cheese

MAKES 8 SERVINGS

16 ounces	dry elbow macaroni
4 tablespoons	butter
1/4 cup	flour
2 cups	whole milk
1 cup	chicken stock or broth
1/2 cup	heavy cream
2 cups	shredded white cheddar cheese
2 cups	shredded Gruyere cheese
2 cups	shredded American cheese
8 strips	thick-sliced bacon, cooked and crumbled, divided
1/2 cup	diced roasted green chiles, divided
1/4 cup	panko or breadcrumbs
1/4 cup	shredded Parmesan cheese

Preheat smoker and add wood following the manufacturer's instructions. Heat to 180 degrees F and lightly grease a 9 x 13-inch metal baking pan.

Prepare macaroni according to package directions, drain and run under cool water; set aside.

In a large saucepan over medium heat, melt butter. Sprinkle with the flour, whisk for 1 minute, and add milk, chicken stock, and cream. Stir in cheddar, Gruyere, and American cheeses, a handful at a time, whisking after each addition until incorporated and sauce is smooth.

Spread half the cooked macaroni in prepared baking pan. Ladle half the cheese sauce evenly over macaroni. Sprinkle evenly with half the bacon and half the chiles. Spoon the rest of the macaroni on top, followed by the remaining bacon and chiles. Ladle the remaining cheese sauce over the top and sprinkle with panko or breadcrumbs and Parmesan cheese. Place the pan in the smoker, close the lid, and smoke for 15 minutes. Increase heat to 375 degrees F and continue cooking until mixture is hot and bubbling and crumb topping is lightly browned, 20 to 30 more minutes. Remove from smoker and cool for 10 minutes before serving.

#88
Smoked Brown Sugar Salmon
MAKES 6 SERVINGS

2 tablespoons	packed brown sugar
1 teaspoon	salt
1 teaspoon	lemon pepper seasoning
1 teaspoon	dried dill weed
2 pounds	fresh salmon fillets
	lemon wedges

In a shallow dish, combine the brown sugar, salt, lemon pepper, and dill. Coat the salmon fillets in the mixture and arrange in a baking dish. Cover and refrigerate for 1 hour.

Preheat smoker and add wood following the manufacturer's instructions. Heat to 275 degrees F. Arrange the salmon fillets on the grill and smoke until the internal temperature reaches 145 degrees, about 1 hour. Let rest for 5 minutes and serve with lemon wedges.

Lemon-Garlic Shrimp

MAKES 4 SERVINGS

30	large shrimp, shelled (tails left on) and deveined
3 tablespoons	All-Around Rub (page 12) or your favorite rub
1/2 cup	butter, melted
2	garlic cloves, minced
1/2	fresh lemon

Preheat smoker and add wood following the manufacturer's instructions. Heat to 275 degrees F and lightly grease a 9 x 13-inch metal baking pan.

Sprinkle shrimp generously on all sides with rub and pat to adhere. Arrange shrimp in rows in the pan. Place the pan in the smoker, close the lid, and cook for 10 minutes.

Combine butter and garlic in a small dish and stir to combine. Turn shrimp over and drizzle with the garlic butter mixture. Continue smoking until shrimp are cooked and opaque, 10 to 15 more minutes. Remove from smoker, cool for 5 minutes, and squeeze fresh lemon over shrimp to serve.

Butter-Basted King Crab Legs

MAKES 3 TO 4 SERVINGS

6 pounds	**king crab legs**
1^1/$_2$ cups	**butter, melted**
^{1}/$_3$ cup	**fresh lemon juice**
1 teaspoon	**fresh lemon zest**
3	**garlic cloves, minced**
1 tablespoon	**salt**
1^1/$_2$ teaspoons	**freshly ground black pepper**
1 teaspoon	**Old Bay seafood seasoning**
	lemon wedges

Preheat smoker and add wood following the manufacturer's instructions. Heat to 250 degrees F.

Use kitchen shears to make a cut up the underside of each crab leg for easier shelling later. In a small bowl, combine the melted butter, lemon juice, lemon zest, garlic, salt, pepper, and Old Bay seasoning. Brush the mixture generously over the crab legs.

Place the crab legs directly on the smoker grill grates, close the lid, and smoke, basting with the butter mixture every 10 minutes, until crab meat is cooked through and opaque, 30 to 40 minutes. Cool for 10 minutes and brush with butter mixture again before serving with fresh lemon wedges.

DESSERTS
&
SWEETS

Caramel-Walnut Cheesecake
MAKES 6 TO 8 SERVINGS

1	single-crust (9-inch) pie dough
8 ounces	cream cheese, softened
$^1/_2$ cup	sugar
4	eggs, room temperature, divided
1 teaspoon	vanilla
1 cup	chopped walnuts
1 jar (12$^1/_4$ ounces)	caramel ice cream topping
	whipped cream, for topping

Preheat smoker and add wood following the manufacturer's instructions. Heat to 325 degrees F.

Fit the pie dough into a 9-inch metal pie pan. In a small bowl, beat cream cheese, sugar, 1 egg, and vanilla until smooth. Spread mixture in pie crust and sprinkle with walnuts. In a medium bowl, whisk remaining eggs and then gradually whisk in caramel topping until blended. Pour evenly over walnuts.

Place the pie pan in smoker, close the lid, and cook until filling is nearly firm and lightly browned, 50 to 70 minutes. (Cover crust edges with aluminum foil strips if they begin to brown too much.) Remove from smoker and cool for 1 hour. Cover and refrigerate at least 4 hours or overnight before slicing. Top with whipped cream before serving.

Smoked Pumpkin Pie

MAKES 6 TO 8 SERVINGS

1	single-crust (9-inch) pie dough
1 can (15 ounces)	pureed pumpkin
1 can (14 ounces)	sweetened condensed milk
2	eggs, beaten
1 teaspoon	cinnamon
1½ teaspoons	pumpkin pie spice
⅛ teaspoon	salt
	whipped cream or ice cream

Preheat smoker and add wood following the manufacturer's instructions. Heat to 325 degrees F. Fit pie dough into a 9-inch metal pie pan and set aside.

In a large bowl, combine the pumpkin, condensed milk, eggs, cinnamon, pumpkin pie spice, and salt. Pour mixture into pie crust.

Place the pie pan in the smoker over indirect heat. Close the lid and smoke until center is set and a knife inserted in center comes out clean, 50 to 60 minutes. Cool on a wire rack to room temperature and serve with whipped cream or ice cream.

Chocolate-Bourbon Pecan Pie

MAKES 8 SERVINGS

1	single-crust (9-inch) pie dough
1¹/₂ cups	pecan halves
6 tablespoons	butter
2 ounces	semisweet chocolate, chopped
³/₄ cup	dark corn syrup
4	eggs, lightly beaten
¹/₂ cup	packed dark brown sugar
1 tablespoon	unsweetened cocoa powder
2 tablespoons	bourbon
¹/₄ teaspoon	salt
	whipped cream or ice cream

Preheat smoker and add wood following the manufacturer's instructions. Heat to 350 degrees F. Fit the pie dough into a 9-inch metal pie plate.

Spread the pecans on a rimmed baking sheet, place in the smoker, close the lid, and cook until lightly toasted and fragrant, stirring once midway through cooking, about 10 minutes. Remove from the smoker and cool.

Meanwhile, melt the butter in a small saucepan over low heat. Add the chocolate and cook, stirring often, until smooth. Remove from the heat and cool. Pour the mixture into a large bowl and add the corn syrup, eggs, brown sugar, cocoa, bourbon, and salt. Stir until combined and pour into the prepared crust. Sprinkle smoked pecans over filling. Set the pie pan on a baking sheet, place in the smoker, and cook until filling is nearly firm, 45 to 55 minutes. Remove from the smoker and cool to room temperature. Cut in slices and serve with whipped cream or ice cream.

Apple Pecan Cake

MAKES 9 SERVINGS

2 cups	Granny Smith apples, peeled and cut in $1/2$-inch pieces (2 to 3 large apples)
1 cup	sugar
$1/2$ cup	vegetable oil
1	egg
$1^1/2$ cups	flour
1 teaspoon	baking soda
$1/2$ teaspoon	cinnamon
$1/4$ teaspoon	salt
$1/2$ cup	chopped pecans

Crumb mixture:

$3/4$ cup	packed brown sugar
$1^1/2$ tablespoons	flour
$1^1/2$ teaspoons	cinnamon
2 tablespoons	cold salted butter

In a medium bowl, sprinkle the apples with the sugar, stir well, and let stand for 30 minutes. Preheat smoker and add wood following the manufacturer's instructions. Heat to 350 degrees F. Grease an 8 x 8-inch metal baking pan.

In a large bowl, combine the oil, egg, flour, baking soda, cinnamon, and salt. Add the apple mixture and pecans, and stir just until combined. Spread into prepared baking pan.

In a small bowl, combine the brown sugar, flour, cinnamon, and butter, cutting in the butter with a fork until crumbs are the size of small peas. Sprinkle the crumb mixture over the cake batter. Put in the smoker, close the lid, and cook until a toothpick inserted in the cake comes out clean, 35 to 45 minutes. Cool on a wire rack before serving.

Peach-Bourbon Skillet Upside-Down Cake

MAKES 6 SERVINGS

For the topping:

2 cups	peeled sliced fresh or frozen and thawed peaches
2 tablespoons	bourbon
1/4 cup	butter, melted
1/2 cup	packed brown sugar

For the cake:

1/2 cup	butter, softened
3/4 cup	sugar
1	egg, room temperature
1 teaspoon	vanilla
1 1/4 cups	flour
1 1/4 teaspoons	baking powder
1/4 teaspoon	salt
1/2 cup	milk
	whipped cream or ice cream

In a medium bowl, combine the peaches and bourbon and let stand for 10 minutes. Preheat smoker and add wood following the manufacturer's instructions. Heat to 350 degrees F.

Pour melted butter in a 10-inch cast iron skillet and sprinkle evenly with brown sugar. Arrange peach slices on top.

In a large bowl, cream the softened butter and sugar with an electric mixer on medium speed until light and fluffy, about 5 minutes. Beat in egg and vanilla. In a medium bowl, whisk flour, baking powder, and salt; add to the butter mixture alternately with milk, beating after each addition just until combined. Spoon batter over peaches and smooth with spatula.

Put the skillet in the smoker, close the lid, and cook until a toothpick inserted in cake comes out clean, 40 to 45 minutes. Remove the skillet from the smoker and cool on a wire rack for 10 minutes. Serve topped with whipped cream or ice cream.

#96

Smoky Chocolate Ganache Sauce

MAKES ABOUT 2 1/4 CUPS

1 1/2 cups **heavy cream**
1/4 teaspoon **cinnamon**
3/4 cup **semisweet chocolate chips**

Preheat smoker and add wood following the manufacturer's instructions. Heat to 275 degrees F.

Combine cream and cinnamon in a medium cast iron skillet and whisk to combine. Add the chocolate chips and place in the smoker. Close the lid and smoke for 15 minutes. Stir to blend, and continue smoking until cream bubbles and chocolate chips are fully melted, 5 to 10 more minutes. Stir until smooth and serve over ice cream or your favorite dessert. Leftover sauce may be stored in a covered container in the refrigerator for up to 1 week.

Smoky Peanut Butter Cup S'mores

MAKES 8 SERVINGS

8 **whole graham crackers**
8 **full-size chocolate peanut butter cups**
8 **large marshmallows**

Preheat smoker and add wood following the manufacturer's instructions. Heat to 275 degrees F.

Line a baking sheet with aluminum foil.

Break each graham cracker in 2 squares. Arrange all of the squares on the prepared baking sheet. Top 8 of the squares with 1 peanut butter cup each and top the other 8 squares with 1 marshmallow each.

Place the baking sheet on the smoker grate over indirect heat. Close the lid and cook until the peanut butter cups begin to melt and the marshmallows start to turn brown and puffy, 15 to 20 minutes.

Carefully flip the marshmallow-topped graham crackers onto the peanut butter cup-topped graham crackers, and push down gently on the toasted marshmallows. Serve immediately.

Brown Sugar Pineapple

MAKES 6 SERVINGS

1	whole fresh ripe pineapple, top, rind, and core removed
1 cup	packed brown sugar
¼ cup	bourbon
¼ cup	maple syrup
1 teaspoon	salt
	vanilla bean ice cream

Preheat smoker and add wood following the manufacturer's instructions. Heat to 250 degrees F.

Pat pineapple dry with paper towels. In a small bowl, combine the brown sugar, bourbon, maple syrup, and salt. Use a pastry brush to brush the mixture all over the outside of the pineapple.

Place the pineapple upright on the grill grates, close the lid, and smoke for 30 minutes. Brush with glaze and continue cooking until pineapple is caramelized, 15 to 20 more minutes. Remove to a cutting board, cool for 5 minutes, and use a sharp knife to cut the pineapple into 1-inch slices. Place slices on smoker grill grates, brush with glaze, and smoke until hot and lightly browned, 10 to 15 more minutes. Remove from smoker, cool for 10 minutes, and serve warm with vanilla bean ice cream.

Smoked Cherry Crisp

MAKES 6 SERVINGS

5 to 6 cups	pitted cherries (fresh or frozen and thawed)
1^1/4 cups	sugar, divided
1 cup	flour
1 teaspoon	baking powder
^{3}/4 teaspoon	salt
1	egg
^{1}/3 cup	unsalted butter, melted
	whipped cream or ice cream

Preheat smoker and add wood following the manufacturer's instructions. Heat to 350 degrees F. Grease an 8 x 8-inch metal baking pan.

In a large bowl, combine the cherries with ^{1}/4 cup of the sugar. Let sit for 10 minutes, and spread cherries in the prepared baking pan.

In a medium bowl, combine flour, remaining 1 cup sugar, baking powder, salt, and egg, and mix just until blended; mixture will be crumbly. Sprinkle mixture evenly over cherries and drizzle with melted butter. Place the pan in the smoker over indirect heat. Close the lid and cook until lightly browned and bubbling, 35 to 45 minutes. Serve warm with whipped cream or ice cream.

The Most Appealing Banana Dessert

MAKES 6 SERVINGS

6	**ripe unpeeled bananas**
¹⁄₂ cup	**semisweet chocolate chips**
¹⁄₂ cup	**miniature marshmallows**
¹⁄₃ cup	**toffee bits**

Preheat smoker and add wood following the manufacturer's instructions. Heat to 350 degrees F. Cut 6 (12-inch) sheets of heavy-duty aluminum foil.

Cut a slit in the inside curve of each banana peel from the stem to the end, being careful not to cut all the way through.

Place each banana in the center of a piece of foil and gently press slits open to form pockets. Divide the chocolate chips, marshmallows, and toffee bits evenly among the bananas, holding while gently pressing ingredients in the pockets. Fold foil around each banana, crimping to seal.

Place the packets directly on the grill grates, close the lid, and cook until bananas are hot and chocolate is melted, 15 to 20 minutes. Remove from smoker, cool for 5 minutes, and serve with forks.

Brown Butter Chocolate Chip Cookies

MAKES 36 COOKIES

1 cup	unsalted butter
1 cup	packed brown sugar
1/3 cup	sugar
2	eggs
2 teaspoons	vanilla
2 cups	flour
1 teaspoon	baking soda
3/4 teaspoon	salt
1 1/2 cups	semisweet chocolate chips
2 (1 1/4-ounce)	chocolate toffee candy bars such as Heath or Skor, chopped roughly into 1/4-inch pieces
	flaky sea salt, for sprinkling (optional)

In a medium saucepan over medium heat, melt the butter and cook, stirring often, until it foams, then browns, 5 to 8 minutes. Pour into a mixing bowl and use a spatula to scrape the brown bits into the bowl; cool for 5 minutes. Add the sugars to the browned butter and beat with an electric mixer on medium speed until blended, about 1 minute. Add the eggs and vanilla and beat on medium-high until mixture thickens, about 1 minute.

In a medium bowl, combine the flour, baking soda, and salt and whisk to blend. Add flour mixture to the egg mixture and stir just until combined. Stir in chocolate chips and toffee pieces until incorporated. Let dough rest, covered, at room temperature for 30 minutes.

Meanwhile, preheat smoker and add wood following the manufacturer's instructions. Heat to 350 degrees F. Line baking sheet with parchment paper.

Scoop the dough in rounded tablespoons, roll lightly into balls, and arrange on prepared baking sheet about 3 inches apart. Flatten tops slightly with fingers. Sprinkle with flaky sea salt if you wish.

Place the baking sheet in the smoker, close the lid, and smoke until the edges of the cookies are lightly browned and firm but the centers are still soft, 12 to 18 minutes. Cool on baking sheet for 3 minutes and transfer to a wire rack to cool completely. Repeat with remaining dough.

NOTES

NOTES

NOTES

NOTES

NOTES

Metric Conversion Chart

VOLUME MEASUREMENTS		WEIGHT MEASUREMENTS		TEMPERATURE CONVERSION	
U.S.	Metric	U.S.	Metric	Fahrenheit	Celsius
1 teaspoon	5 ml	1/2 ounce	15 g	250	120
1 tablespoon	15 ml	1 ounce	30 g	300	150
1/4 cup	60 ml	3 ounces	90 g	325	160
1/3 cup	75 ml	4 ounces	115 g	350	180
1/2 cup	125 ml	8 ounces	225 g	375	190
2/3 cup	150 ml	12 ounces	350 g	400	200
3/4 cup	175 ml	1 pound	450 g	425	220
1 cup	250 ml	2 1/4 pounds	1 kg	450	230

MORE 101 THINGS® IN THESE
FAVORITES

BACON
CAKE MIX
CASSEROLE
RAMEN NOODLES
SLOW COOKER

Each 128 pages, $12.99

Available at bookstores or directly from Gibbs Smith
1.800.835.4993
www.gibbs-smith.com

Gibbs Smith

About the Author

Eliza Cross is an award-winning writer and the author of 17 books, including the bestselling *Bacon*, *Beans and Beer* and *Small Bites*. She is the founder of the BENSA Bacon Lovers Society, an E.A.T. certified food judge, and a food blogger. She lives with her family near Denver, Colorado.